Eyes that See

How do we know it is God who is speaking to us? It might be our imagination, it could even be the devil. What about the prophecy that was given in church last Sunday? There is so much happening today; changes in church services, new churches and groups of churches being formed, new theologies and concepts of the church and its mission. How can we sort out what is of God?

Douglas McBain seeks to answer these and many other questions through Biblical teaching, and drawing on his pastoral experience in three churches and his experience in an ininerant ministry in five continents as Director of Manna Ministries trust.

This book fills an urgent gap in contemporary Christian writing.

Clifford Fryer
1986

We have needed for a long time a clearly and decisively written book on discernment. This is it. This book should be widely read.

Michael Harper
1986

All Scripture references are taken from the New International Version of the Bible unless otherwise stated.

Renewal Issues in the Church

Eyes that See

The Spiritual Gift of Discernment

Douglas McBain

Marshall Pickering

To Christine with love

Marshall Morgan and Scott
Marshall Pickering
3 Beggarwood Lane, Basingstoke, Hants RG23 7LP, UK

Copyright © 1986 by Douglas McBain
First published in 1986 by Marshall Morgan and Scott
Publications Ltd
Part of the Marshall Pickering Holdings Group
A subsidiary of the Zondervan Corporation

ISBN 0 551 01389 3

Printed in Great Britain by
The Camelot Press, Southampton, Hants

Contents

Author's Preface   vii

1 The Spiritual Gift of Discernment   1

2 The Nature of Discernment   16

3 Discernment and Signs and Wonders   28

4 Discernment and Healing   42

5 Discernment and the Ministry of Deliverance   59

6 Discernment and Scripture   73

7 Discernment and Relevations   87

8 Discerning God's Will in Guidance   103

9 Discerning Christ's Church   118

10 God's Discerning Man   136

Further Reading   148

Author's Preface

The argument as to whether or not the gifts of the Holy Spirit are for today is now just about over. There must be very few who still hold to the position that charismatic gifts were only for the early Church. Their argument is based upon a distinction between what is temporary and what is permanent that is very dubious indeed. For the most part we are satisfied that God has many creative new gifts to grant to His children. The various gift lists in the New Testament are neither exclusive nor conclusive, but provide the raw material out of which an infinite variety of new charismatic permutations are possible for the people of God.

In the light of this, why is it that the gift and ministry of discernment is such a neglected Cinderella? It could be that our modern stress on immediacy in our relationship with God has diminished the value of serious reflection. Maybe our concentration on the spiritual is creating an unworthy suspicion of the intellectual. Perhaps it is simply that the concept of power is always more attractive than that of truth.

In what follows I am attempting to find a better balance than this. Power without integrity always corrupts. I write as a committed advocate for renewal in the Holy Spirit. From time to time I have been privileged to see some remarkable signs of God at work. I believe that the Holy Spirit is continuing to renew the Church at this time and that we all need much more of Him. I have faith to believe that my generation is only seeing the beginnings of all this, whilst it is probable that today's children will live to see the fullest outflow of the Holy Spirit worldwide since Pentecost. For these things to happen it is essential that we add level heads to our warmer hearts. God will never be satisfied with us if we settle for less than the best. Since all that charismatically glitters is not spiritual gold we will need to become much more discerning in the process than we are at present.

I am grateful to many friends who have helped me both in the immediate task of this book and also in my ongoing spiritual pilgrimage. As must be obvious to all of them I have so much more to learn. What a joy it is to have Tom Smail living nearby again. He and I have been close friends for years and his constructive comments like his strong friendship have given immense encouragement. This is also true of Clifford Fryer, at one time my associate in Streatham, and still a trusted colleague. The Manna office staff have been a constant source of support. In particular I am grateful to Ian and Helen Collinge, Brian Swain my administrator, and Rosemary Tijou who has paintstakingly typed and corrected the manuscript. My heartfelt thanks to Alison and Alec, Elspeth, Janet and Graham for being the children they are to me. To my dear elderly parents who still maintain a lively interest in the activities of their youngest son. And above all, to my most caring, supportive and loving friend, Christine my wife. She holds my life, my work and our family together in a unique and precious way.

I hope that this offering will stimulate our search for both the gifts and graces of the Holy Spirit who holds all things in mature balance. The same must be possible for those whom He inspires. If my contribution causes us to seek the One who is the focus for all the Spirit's activity I will be more than satisfied. As we find Him, follow Him and reveal Him to others He will bless us increasingly with 'Eyes that See'.

Douglas McBain
Manna Ministries Trust
484 King's Road, London, SW10 0LF.

1986

1

The Spiritual Gift of Discernment

She was sitting in the seat nearest the centre aisle. The nervous young man was about to preach one of his first sermons. Before he could begin, God spoke to him clearly, precisely and wholly unexpectedly. 'That is your future wife sitting down there – the attractive blonde, wearing nurses' shoes!' How the sermon went over that night paled into insignificance in the light of this dramatic personal revelation. They did not meet each other for many months. When they did, at the local hospital where she was nursing his father, the rest was a foregone conclusion. Twenty-nine years married and four children further on, mutual love has continued in the same way for Christine and me. We came together through recognising and responding to the voice of a Father who loves to surprise His family with His plans.

Discernment has to do with identifying communications that come from God. Not all of them are of the same obvious significance as this romantic reminiscence. Nevertheless, all of us constantly need to hear God speak for ourselves. Many of our insights immediately affect our attitudes to others and, consequently, our relationships with them. They create the bias that sets up our inner disposition. Discernment is also a necessary corporate quality to be exercised by the whole Church. I cannot think of a more necessary gift for the present-day Church than this. It is true that gloomy prognostications about the future of the Church have now given way to more morale-boosting optimism. Yet it will require much wisdom for the Church as a whole if we are to see significant growth in our personal experience of God's Spirit balanced by a new maturity in under-standing, compassion in ministry and effectiveness in mission. It is a discerning Church which is a healthy Church and God has much more to impart to us.

The subjects we are going to take up deal with some of the issues where pressures are most keenly felt. In this chapter and the next I am attempting to open up the grounds for a ministry of discernment and indicate what that really means. With matters to do with the supernatural once more on the agenda for many Christians, we need to survey signs and wonders, and the ministries of healing and deliverance, both of which have suffered from demythologising in the past and now, I fear, remythologising in the present. When new things are happening, there is always a fresh appeal to Scripture. What then are its true intentions? What about the place for such special revelations as the incident I have just described? They may be very important to us but how can we test out visions, inner convictions, words of prophecy, words of knowledge and the like? How can we be sure that it's more than a matter of our own imagination getting the better of us? What kind of Church is it that can cope with these things without on the one hand despising them or on the other ignoring the need for careful judg-ment? What kind of person is the man who 'gets wisdom and also understanding, discernment and sound judgment?' I hope to show that it is the finest and tenderest Church and the wisest and most attractively open person who is so blessed, 'A boy in my father's house' (Proverbs 4:3). God loves to bless His children with wisdom characterised by its given-ness.

Scriptural Introductions

The search for wisdom is as old as mankind itself. Among the ancient Greeks the renowned philosopher Plato saw wisdom as the greatest of all our virtues. But to the Hebrew people whose understanding is reflected in the Bible, wisdom was expressed in more down to earth terms. Instead of being confined to an abstract realm of concepts it had more to do with understanding the complex problems of life. A wise man is one who has the necessary skill in successfully mastering life's ground rules. A foolish man is one who has little or no idea how to cope. He does not learn the lessons that experience teaches. This is the teaching of the Book of Proverbs which is an incisive and witty primer in the art of getting on. Perhaps we could think of it as the first of a long line of books on 'ten easy steps to success'. Such guides are always popular. In contrast to many of its present day *How to . . .* successors however, the book of Proverbs is much more reliable. For wisdom does lead to success but also to good behaviour. The wise person has learnt to curb his tongue. He manages his time well. He is bearable in the early morning, and also in times of sickness or sadness. Shrewd thoughts, noble deeds, and apt remarks betray wisdom's presence. Wisdom is written into the universe itself. This teaching which is also reflected in some of the Psalms and in the books of Job and Ecclesiastes, has a profound impact throughout the rest of the Scriptures. It affects the prophets in the Old Testament and the apostles in the New. It lays down the foundations for our understanding of the meaning of discernment. When it comes to describing Christ in His relationship to God and to Creation, and to the whole treasury of wisdom and knowledge, it is to the Book of Proverbs that the New Testament writers turn. For the Bible teaches us that Christ Himself is wisdom and wisdom itself is found only in Christ. Right at the very beginning of our study we can see some important principles about discernment. Proverbs tells us that it is God's most practical gift for the spiritually minded. True discernments

like godly wisdom are always earthed in the everyday. Yet
Jesus is the supreme example of active discernment. He
possesses all wisdom and distributes all insight. There can
never be a more powerful demonstration of discernment in
us than when we reveal the mind of Christ to others.

Through Relationship

Wisdom is not just an ideal to be highly prized because it
is rarely seen. The Bible teaches that it is fully available to
those who ask for it. In Proverbs we are reminded on several
occasions that to make a start at acquiring wisdom we must
begin with a right relationship with God. For 'The fear of
the Lord is the beginning of wisdom', (1.7; 9.10; 15.33).
When we come to the Lord with glad and worshipful
submission He will grant wisdom to us. We will never gain
true wisdom outside of this relationship. The message of
Genesis 3 is the sad commentary of what happens to those
who go for a fruit 'desirable for gaining wisdom' (Genesis
3.5). They flout this first principle. Adam and Eve went
about getting wisdom their own way and the Bible tells us
of the disastrous consequences which have followed ever
since. One small step for them was one catastrophic leap
for mankind. Their precocious search led to man's fall, our
sinfulness and estrangement from God, our folly, much
endless frustration and ultimately death itself. All these
consequences are with us still to this day through the foolish-
ness of sin. In the absence of this living relationship with
God our journey through life is bound to follow the same
dismal route.

The pithy style of Proverbs is echoed by the New Testament writer James. 'If any of you lack wisdom, he should
ask God who gives generously to all without finding fault
and it will be given him' (1.5). He shows us that faith is a
vital element in our relationship with God. 'But when he
asks, he must believe and not doubt, because he who doubts
is like a wave of the sea blown and tossed by the wind. That
man shall not think that he will receive anything from the

Lord, he is a double minded man, unstable in all he does' (1.6–8). God rewards unwavering faith. He gave Stephen understanding of His purposes for Israel as he suffered murderous inquisition at the hands of Israel's religious leaders. He gave Paul special understanding of His revealed word. Even the great apostle could not have ministered to the world without this. It is crystal clear that God will make this readily available to us as well, as we go to Him for it in faith.

A Spiritual Gift For All

Wisdom and insight are not to be thought of as the sole preserve of church leaders who do require these qualities in a special way because of the nature of their responsibilities. But God gives wisdom to all who ask Him for it. One of the most treasured expressions of this is in the gift of discernment or 'the ability to distinguish between the spirits', to which Paul refers in his list of gifts in the first letter to the Corinthians (1 Cor: 12.10). It is quite plain that it is a gift of the highest value. Even though it is named as such only once in Scripture, as I hope will become increasingly plain as we go on, its manifestations are many and varied. Its applications are always important. Christian people always stand in need of discernment.

The phrase 'to distinguish between Spirits' means to be able to separate spiritual manifestations at the point of their origins. The main word *diakrisis* or *anakrisis* is a compound word taken from the verb *krinein*, which carries the idea of separating, sifting, distinguishing, and even in some instances in a legal sense – condemning. The person who discerns has a special capacity to weigh things up and draw all the right conclusions from them. There are many more gifts than the nine mentioned in Corinthians which should not be regarded as a final list of the fresh abilities God has available for us. In common with all the other gifts discernment is a *charism* which means that it has its origin in the grace of God rather than in our natural ability. God in His grace will grant us discernment. It is also one of *'the spirituals'* (1 Corinthians 12.1), operating only by means of the inspiration of the Holy Spirit. Among these gifts are those which lead to powerful deeds like the gifts of faith or healing, or miraculous powers. There are also gifts which release us in our worship like the gift of tongues and its partner the gift of interpretation. But the gift of discernment belongs to a cluster together with prophecy, words of wisdom and knowledge which are all to do with God's desire to give us special revelation. Discernment is the means by which we can identify the source of any spiritual manifestation which may be one of three kinds.

Firstly, the manifestation may be from God Himself. For to our circumscribed thinking it does appear as if He has strange ways of revealing His Will and purpose from time to time. His ways cannot be limited either by our understanding or our experience or expectations. Sometimes we have great difficulty in recognising them. This is especially true when God leads us through times of difficulty, pressure or stress. The patriarch Joseph shows us his discernment when he reflects on all the awful experiences which he has gone through which were apparently due to the unkind jealousy of his brothers. 'You intended to harm me' he declares, 'but God intended it for good to accomplish what is now being done, the saving of many lives.' (Genesis 50.20).

Secondly, the manifestation may be from the devil. From time to time Satan will even come to us masquerading as an angel of light, (2 Corinthians 11.14). His servants also like to make similar appearances but providing we are armed with discernment we will not be hoodwinked by their dazzling displays even when they make a convincing show of being the all star smarmy servants of righteousness. With discernment this too is just a trick that we can see through. *Or thirdly, it may be that the source of the manifestation is only human after all.* For as students of psychology and other related sciences of human behaviour tell us, we ourselves are sometimes capable of the most unusual things.

Christian people are often not sufficiently aware of the variety of our mental and spiritual gymnastics and of the strange conclusions to which they may lead. We should not be too eager to brand all that is unusual but not of God as being of the devil. Strange perceptions, telepathic communications and the like can also belong to our natural human condition. They illustrate the fact that beneath the conscious-levels of the mind of each one of us there lie vast unexplored continents in which all sorts of mental powers exist producing some remarkable effects. An acute sense of discernment will indicate to us the source of any manifestation. It will also enable us to distinguish the extent to which natural and spiritual factors combine in it. All spiritual gifts are released to others through the medium of our own humanity, for it is always true that we have this treasure in clay pots. Even the most spiritual Christians will transmit the inspiration of the Holy Spirit through the filter of their own understanding. But gifted with *diakrisis* we are able to make a wise and accurate judgment on this.

Far from this gift being of the second sight kind however, we need to notice that Paul locates it squarely as a *gift for the Body of Christ*. The sphere of its operation is set amongst those who are in Christ and also in established and caring relationships to one another. It is granted to Christians in this way 'for their common good' (1 Corinthians 12.7), Paul says. It brings corporate blessings. We build each other up by its manifestation rather than pull each other down. The purpose of the exercise of the gift is to express loving service to those who receive it (1 Corinthians 12.4). It is also described as a 'working'. Armed with discernment we are able to penetrate through the outer camouflage of another's actions, words or attitudes to the level of intention and motive. So the result of the exercise of the gift is that the whole Body of Christ is mightily blessed and properly equipped for service for Christ.

Jesus and Discernment

As with all spiritual gifts Jesus Himself is the best exponent. If we want to see them operating in a balanced way then it is to the Gospels that we must turn as we see the powerful effectiveness of Christ's life and ministry described there. From His teaching to His disciples we soon notice the high priority He places on wisdom. He draws a sharp contrast between wisdom and folly and His condemnation of all forms of spiritual ineptitude is sharp. Hence the parable of the wise and foolish builders, whose houses are built on either rock or sand (Matthew 7.24–27). It is only wisdom to build our lives on the practice of the word of Jesus. For according to Jesus wisdom comes as a result of our willingness to listen to His teaching, as it were, with our inward ears. Hearing without application is the height of folly for it leads to a hard heart and spiritual emptiness. It is to be hoped that today the numbers of those who listen to the Word of God in this way is declining. Roast preacher at Sunday lunch is not an appetising menu! Those who feed on this sort of diet through attacking and destroying both the messenger and his message never show many signs of spiritual growth. We must first hear God's Word and then go forth to do it. Moreover, the disciples of Jesus are to develop a capacity for shrewdness and gumption in their daily living. This is the point He is making in the parable of the unjust steward who is also an astute manager (Luke 16.1–9). The point of the teaching is to impart an eminently practical lesson on money. Instead of wasting financial resources on ourselves or on others we are to put them to the best possible use by gaining the friendship of those who will be eternally grateful to us for the way we have served them. Jesus is insisting that mission is a wise investment for money, and His comments are still entirely appropriate for the Church of God today. 'The people of this world are more shrewd in dealing with their own kind than are the people of light' (Luke 16.8).

This theme of the need for insight and understanding is

emphasised again at the commissioning of the twelve for kingdom ministry (Matthew 10:1ff). This is to be a powerful extension of His own ministry but He will accomplish it through them. They will drive out the demons and cure sicknesses in His Name (Matthew 10.1). They will raise the dead, cleanse the lepers and preach the message of the kingdom (Matthew 10.7–8). They will move out in mission motivated by gratitude, freely giving because they have freely received. They go in faith that the Father will provide all that they could ever need (Matthew 10.8–9). Yet for all this, their mission is not to be undertaken with naivety. They go with the harmlessness of sheep amongst wolves and with the innocence of the dove too. They also go with the thoughtfulness of the snake though lacking its venom (Matthew 10.16). In the special way that only Jesus makes possible, they are to engage in their mission with a penetrating understanding of the motives of those who will oppose them. Thus prepared and armed, Jesus adds this reassuring word 'but when they arrest you, do not worry about what to say or how to say it. *At that time* you will be given what to say, for it will not be you speaking but the Spirit of your Father through you' (Matthew 10.19).

So far as Jesus is concerned, this matter of discerning the right words and expressing them in the right way is a gift and in this He agrees with the teaching of both the Old Testament and the rest of the New Testament. True insight is not through our own intelligence or perception alone. Our minds need to be nourished on a healthy diet of Scripture but in fact, God grants us the capacity at the appropriate time often in a miraculous way. It is the experience of the gift of discernment which confirms our status as God's children. This is the context of Jesus' expression of praise, thanksgiving and joy at the conclusion of the first mission by the twelve soon followed by the mission of the seventy-two (Luke 10.21–24). It is because He sees that His Father, the Lord of Heaven has hidden these things from the wise and prudent and revealed them to those who are childlike in their trust. If they have God's insight it is because they are His children, but if they are dull and blind to what God says then this shows that they have never really belonged to Him in the first place. Herein lies the paradox which is in all spiritual wisdom. People who are wise in their own eyes never receive discernment. But if we are trusting and open to God, we will perceive all things, even the hidden mysteries of God.

The mission of the seventy-two teaches us much about the true nature of our evangelistic task and much more besides. It is important to see that at the beginning Jesus instructs His disciples to start their ministry with the prayer that others may join them in the work. He told them that 'the harvest is plentiful but the workers are few. Ask the Lord of the harvest therefore, to send out workers into His harvest field', (Luke 10.2). It is at their return that Jesus brings us to the high point of all discernment. The climax is not in the vision of a harvest with which evangelism should always begin but in the revelation of God Himself to which all evangelism should lead. So Jesus says 'all things have been committed to Me by My Father. No one knows who the Son is except the Father, and no one knows who the Father is except the Son and those to whom the Son chooses to reveal Him' (Luke 10.22). To know Him is to begin to understand Him, His works and ways. It is only as we engage in the dangerous and demanding task of venture for Christ that we will come to this insight. It is those who are obedient to Christ's call who can expect to be inspired by Him with all His treasures of wisdom and knowledge. It is as they are engaged in this task that they receive it.

In this respect the point that Jesus is registering is that the experience of His children is identical to His own. He makes it plain that for Him too it is only as He receives understanding from His Father that He engages in His ministry and also that only as He does the Father's bidding that He gains understanding. Without special revelation personally received He declares that He can do nothing by Himself (John 5.19). All wisdom, knowledge and understanding are communications from the Father. When He sees what the Father is doing He is perfectly clear as to what He has to do, and because the Father loves the Son, He is ready to show Him these things.

This principle of ministry was brought home to me very vividly some years ago. I was travelling to Malaysia on a teaching mission with a good friend Father Ian Petit, a Benedictine monk. Baptist ministers and Benedictine monks are not the most usual members of a joint teaching team but God had brought us together even though we were an improbable duo. Neither of us had visited the countries of South-East Asia to which we were travelling. However, we knew that we would have a time of rich enjoyment and fruitfulness from the start, when we found that we had both been guided to John 5.19 as the basis for our ministry. Practically speaking it meant that the first thing we had to do as we arrived at the various assignments in East and West Malaysia, was to perceive what the Father was already doing there. It was no use sharing our own thoughts however well prepared they seemed to be to us. Once we had seen what our Father was doing we felt confident that He would bless all that we did which mirrored the revelation we had received. We found that this was indeed the case. We also discovered that whilst there was a broad harmony within His purposes at that time in renewing His people, there were also widely differing stages of development in their experience. I have to confess that the Lord gave me an additional spur to developing this attitude of dependence upon Him. Finding that in my hasty packing I had left out my own recently written sermon notes meant that when I stood up to preach it really was a case of 'nothing in my hand I bring, simply to Thy cross I cling'. The truth was that the absence of the notes did not seem to diminish the value of the teaching. Perhaps in some instances the teaching actually improved, although I would not wish to make a case for always preaching on the basis of immediate inspiration rather than after prayerful preparation.

In order to receive accurate understanding for this for ourselves, Jesus makes it plain that there is a further primary step for us. Discernment comes through revelation and as a gift of the Holy Spirit. But repentance is also a vital prerequisite. This is the word with which He begins His public ministry of announcing the Good News of the Kingdom (Mark 1.15). He returns to it frequently throughout the course of His teaching (Matthew 21.32, Mark 6.12, Luke 15.7). It is the key to the forgiveness which He is glad to bestow on all those who hear His message (Luke 24.47). To repent is literally *to change our mind*. It means that we adopt a different mental approach towards ourselves and others and especially toward God. Repentance is not just a miserable sorrow over sin. That can lead to a wallowing attitude which partly enjoys guiltiness. We are genuinely sorry about the sinfulness of our own hearts. I fear that those of us who are evangelical preachers have often been quite happy to bring people to this point without realising the positive qualities which mark genuine repentance. The change of mind of true repentance leads to a fresh openness to the grace of God. Instead of thinking that somehow we can work everything out by ourselves we see that it is only as God enables us that we can get things right.

Renewal Needs Discernment

Receiving wisdom from God was never more needed than it is today when the Church is undergoing the ferment caused by the profoundly renewing work of the Spirit. The hallmark of what God has been doing is in the fresh emphasis He has been laying upon the Holy Spirit and His gifts. The positive impact of the renewal has been immense and still continues to gather spiritual momentum. There are many reasons for supposing that the major consequences in terms of profoundly effective evangelism and prophetic mission are yet to follow. If they happen then the next decades are likely to be amongst the most exciting periods for growth and development that the Christian Church has ever known. It is likely that the Church of the East in Asia and of the South in Africa and Latin America will continue to lead the way. The Churches of the West are not likely to be the leaders though this has often been the way we have thought of them. At the present time we are still trailing behind the newer churches of the third world where the Holy Spirit is moving with greater freedom and power and much greater effectiveness. But every renewal is the rediscovery of an emphasis of the Gospel that has been suffering from neglect. With that rediscovery there is an inbuilt tendency to extremes which in themselves can be as dangerous as was the former neglect through which the truth has been lost from sight. Because of this pendulum factor we are always in need of the insight that comes with accurate discernment.

It is not my purpose at this point to describe all the characteristics of all the different tendencies to extremism which I have encountered in a movement which remains nonetheless essentially healthy. However, there are two dominating dangers which do need our attention.

The first is in the tendency to introspection which controls the climate of life for many charismatic Christians and not a few church fellowships as well. Because of this tendency every time of worship is measured by the pitch of the individual emotions that it manages to stir up. Every offer of ministry is taken up almost always by the same people with the same range of personal problems. Instead of the church being characterised by the awesomeness of its worship or by the adventure in its mission there is a soggy sense of self absorption in the air. As far as matters for intercession are concerned, God's blessing is only sought for 'me and my wife, my John and his wife, us four, no more!' And such an exclusive inward concern can never be right for the Church of the living God. It is not just that it is all so utterly selfish, it is also so tragically boring.

The second is in the form of a somewhat superficial philosophy of pragmatism which is adopted by some without much further consideration. Pragmatism teaches us that everything is valued solely in terms of its practical effectiveness. There is plenty of room for this emphasis in the Church of

God as a whole. We are constantly in need of checking our
actions and our traditions by their effectiveness. But it is
dangerous if results are the only way by which we can
measure truth. Then the justification for every activity is
success and very often immediate success at that. If there
are ways by which people can be healed albeit temporarily
or partially, or congregations increased in number or mighty
miracles experienced, then these ways are followed without
any further question. The thing works and therefore it must
be right. John gives us different criteria for drawing our
conclusions about the rightness or wrongness of any word
or deed which claims Christ's blessing. 'Dear Friends, do
not believe every spirit but test the spirits to see whether
they are from God, because many false prophets have gone
out into the world. This is how you can recognise the Spirit
of God. Every spirit that acknowledges that Jesus Christ
has come in the flesh is from God. But every spirit that does
not acknowledge Jesus is not from God. This is the spirit
of the anti-Christ. . . .'

The worth of our deeds and our spirits is to be assessed
in the light of what they say of Christ's incarnation and
lordship. It is the witness we bring to Him alone that establishes our credibility. Exciting testimonies which are
combined with exaggerated reports which are never
adequately tested out say little of Christ at all. Unfortunately because they are based more on distortion than
reality they usually lead on to awful despair and cynicism
later on as a penalty for our gullibility. Armed with gifts of
discernment we dare to take a more cautious line when
great swelling claims are being made.

We are to test the spirits to see whether they are of God.
We will look for the signs of God's activity and not be taken
in by what may be no more than a spectacular demonstration. We will recall that the Christ who heals is also the
Christ who suffers. The devil is always prepared to give
plenty away to us if he can first secure the primary place in
our devotions (Luke 4.6). In an age which has exalted
success to the highest position we will discern its dangers.

In God's economy there are always other factors to be taken into account lest we should become conceited through our 'surpassingly great revelations' (2 Corinthians 12.7). Our first question is never about how something works but whether it is in accordance with God's revelation in Christ and in Scripture, and in the experience of the people of God as it is attested throughout two millenia.

The dangers caused by a tendency to inwardness in the Church and an undue stress on pragmatism at the expense of truth emphasise the need for discernment today. So too do the complexities that come from an increasingly godless age. The Church in the West is an easy prey to the anti-christ spirits of consumerism and materialism. The latest odd deviation being advocated by a few teachers of the so called prosperity Gospel is a bizarre example of what happens when those who treasure the teachings of the Bible miss its great principles of justice, righteousness and mission. A godless age approves of the more self gratifying alternatives of lots of health and wealth. With God-given wisdom however, we will maintain a wider perspective that is also much more independent of immediate trends like this.

With the aid of a gift of discernment we can see that we are much in need of a renewal of moral toughness. Taking up the cross is at the heart of Christ's call to discipleship. We need to repent of all our follies and excesses if we are truly to believe the Gospel and to follow Him. Christ is the standard by whom we must tell all our actions. Our fresh obedience to Him will also be the key to discovering what it will mean to become God's prophetic people in a world bewildered by its own bitterness.

2

The Nature of Discernment

Through His Spirit Christ makes all His treasures of wisdom and understanding available to us. It is a sign of genuine spiritual growth when we have 'the full riches of complete understanding' (Colossians 2.2–3). He does not expect His people to behave naively even though they are to preserve their souls in innocence. We can confidently affirm that it is the purpose of Christ for His people to possess all the wisdom they need for their salvation and for their service for God. He blesses churches that are wise. Unwise churches without any sense of direction, purpose or awareness of the resources available to them receive Christ's censure. Similarly, there is no excuse for the individual Christian who meanders from one crisis of indecision to another, through a lack of wisdom or understanding. Having considered the need for discernment and have seen that it is a vital gift for us all, we must now come to understand the essential characteristics of discernment as the Scriptures describe them.

Elements in Discernment

a) *The first is the capacity for penetrating observation which Jesus frequently manifested*. When He first encountered Simon Peter (John 1.42) at one glance He took in both Peter's character and also his destiny. The verb here *emble-peim* means to fix one's gaze upon, and John is telling us that Jesus missed nothing as He met with Peter. It is the same a little while later when He meets Nathaniel for the first time, and describes him as 'a true Israelite in whom there is nothing false' (1.47). On the occasion when He healed the paralytic we are told that 'Jesus knew in His spirit what those around Him were thinking in their hearts' (Mark 2.8), so He directed His ministry accordingly in a way that would bring to light their real hidden attitudes. These are just a few examples and there are many others from which we may deduce that Jesus habitually read the minds of those to whom He was talking. Perhaps He also observed what we call body language today. Signs of stress or signs of peace written into the ways in which we use our hands, the lines on our faces and particularly the look in our eyes as 'the lamp of the body', He would immediately see. Certainly He was an expert in understanding the message of our general demeanour.

There is more to His discernment and ours than this, but we need to begin with things that are obvious or we run the danger of missing them altogether. Discernment is a spiritual gift with a large element of supernatural inspiration to it, but it is not without natural and more ordinary elements. Some people have a natural ability for panoramic vision. When they enter a room they take in all the details of what they see, even when they are scarcely conscious of doing so. This is a helpful factor in our spiritual ministry and must be cultivated. Less obviously spiritual signals regularly communicate important information. For instance, we can usually tell when we have come into the company of two people who are very much in love. Without a word being uttered we pick up the unspoken message in the atmosphere between them. We also know when we are walking into a house where there is a great deal of tension, or where the atmosphere is heavy because of the anger which is felt between the various people there. I recall once going to preach in a church which was just on the point of sacking its pastor most unjustly. I had already thought it likely that demonic elements were at work in that situation. When I

entered the vestry before the morning service and met the
tense and angry leaders of the church I knew it for certain.
For if they were like this in the presence of a visitor, what
would they be like when they were not on their best behaviour? On this occasion at least, their mood had not been
created by my message. The service had not even begun. It
was the presence of a negative and destructive force that
was creating these awful group dynamics. Jesus also picked
up these unspoken messages which betray the presence of
a spirit that is unclean or lame or violent. Even in my
limited experience I have also identified spirits of suspicion,
hostility, fear and anger. They can never remain hidden for
long, even though our culture demands that we attempt a
cover up for the sake of good manners.

   b) *Discernment includes perception*. We may be able to
observe all the various things that are going on, but there
is also an *intuitive element* in taking us to the point of
comprehension, to which we now come. Jesus manifested
such intuition throughout his ministry. 'He did not need
man's testimony about man for He knew what was in man'
(John 2.25). For example, when He meets the Samaritan
woman in Sychar he makes her face the truth *He* has already
grasped but which *she* has tried to hide. She declares that
she has no husband to bring back to Jesus. He replies to
her 'The fact is, you have had five husbands and the man
you have is not your husband. What you have said is quite
true' (John 4.18). It is the same when He speaks to Judas
the betrayer at the Last Supper (John 13.27) as well as many
other examples of this in Christ's ministry.

   It is this same quality of perception that we are told about
on many other occasions in the Bible. In the story of Moses
and the triumph of his faith in Hebrews 11 we are encour-
aged to share in the ongoing life of Christian pilgrimage
together with all the people of God in the Old Covenant
and with Jesus Himself. It is indeed a considerable aid to
our understanding of the message of the whole of the Letter
to the Hebrews when we see that the examples culled from
the ancient history of Israel are mostly taken from their

experience of pilgrimage. The ongoing experience of the people of God as they travel from Egypt to Canaan forms a relevant model for our own. Moses made his great decisions on the ground of his spiritual perceptions. 'Looking ahead to his reward' he left Egypt, going off on his incredible safari of faith through the Wilderness as the leader of a rabble of runaway slaves we are told that he persevered because 'He saw Him who is invisible' (Hebrews 11.27). Discernment is the gift through which we also see God. In an age when He is not too visible to most Christian people this is a perception which we all require. When our Christian pilgrimage requires perseverance we need such a gift as this in order to follow God in all His ways. For the truth about God's guidance is that sometimes it is not all that marvellously clear for us to see. As the Psalmist puts it 'Your path leads through the sea, your way through the mighty waters though your footprints were not seen' (Psalm 77.19).

c) *There is a quality of discrimination between similar manifestations of the gift.* It gives the ability to spot the differences. In Hebrews 5.14 we are told that mature Christians demonstrate this because they have fed upon an adequate diet in the Word of God. Through learning how to digest its solid food they have trained themselves 'to distinguish good from evil.' That is to say that they have moved on from the liquid diet of repentance from dead works and faith in God and the other foundational foods mentioned later on, to a real understanding of the facts of Christ's present ministry as our High Priest in heaven. From this they have grasped the implications for their daily living. Their faculties are trained by practice so that as a consequence they manifest strong faith, a sure hope and vigorous service (see 6.1; 6.12,19; 10.19).

It is by this means that we spot whether the source of any manifestation is godly, human or demonic. It is also the way by which we spot where those elements merge. We will look at the issue of demonic bondage in closer detail later on but to take one example may be helpful here. The incident is recorded in Acts 16.16ff. Paul's heated response when he dealt with the young girl in occult bondage in Philippi was not directed to the girl herself. The account points in fact to an opposite conclusion because of Paul's ability to discriminate here. Since the young girl needed the comfort and care vital for those who are infested with evil spirits Paul tolerated her strange testimony for several days. On no other occasion do we find him or others taking their time like this. Jesus Himself insisted that He had given us such authority over the demonic that we can trample on them without being hurt in the process (see Luke 10.19). That is hardly an invitation to procrastination. Having once established a link with the girl however, the moment for expulsion follows and the girl is freed immediately.

Times when spiritual gifts and ministries are being restored to the Church are thrilling times indeed. They are also times when there is much counterfeit satanic activity around calling for this quality of careful discrimination. Jesus warns us frequently of the dangers of false prophets. For it is by means of spectacular ministries that many charlatans will seek to lead Christ's own people astray in the end days (Mark 13.22). It is a fact that Satan persistently imitates even the most beautiful activities of the Holy Spirit for his own ends. His servants seldom begin their work with an all out frontal attack upon the truth of Christ. They do not advertise their presence. Often they preserve some elements of the truth whilst they pursue other elements of obvious error. We need the gift to separate these things out, especially when we are attempting to help those who have slipped into spiritual bondage. We need it when we are unmasking the practical heresies of the hypocrites too (Matthew 23.16). We need to be able to see the point at which wrong motives turn good actions into bad ones worthy of the damnation of hell (Matthew 23.33). Such a gift of discernment will be of great help to others. It may also be a useful check for our own spirits. For who can say that we have never been guilty of putting on a mask and acting a part in order to appear better than we are? Either way we need to notice that in order to develop the gift we need to thoroughly digest the teaching of Scripture.

d) *True discernment leads to accurate interpretations in order to read situations aright*. There are too many examples around us of an incorrect reading of the situation that may well have been rightly diagnosed for us to be content with our present knowledge of these things. Our problem is not, however, entirely new to these days. Paul faced similar difficulties. He tells us of the conviction which God had already given him on many occasions of how he must go to Jerusalem and that this will lead to a time of great personal trial and hardship (Acts 20.22). In spite of the promise of those sufferings, he tells the elders at Ephesus that he must go to Jerusalem and that there is no alternative. When he arrives at Caesarea en route he stays with the evangelist Philip whose four daughters all prophesy, and to make the party complete, the well known prophet Agabus also turns up. Taking Paul's belt he gives a most definite word about what the future holds for its owner at the hands of the Jews in Jerusalem. Although none of these things deter Paul from his purpose, in the next few verses we are told of the way in which the others responded, including in all probability the writer of the account, Luke himself. The prophetic word was clear to them all, but personal preference lead them all to propose an alternative response which undoubtedly would have caused much confusion had it been followed. Armed with a well developed gift of discernment, what was a problem for Luke was no difficulty to Paul. 'I am ready to go' he says, and Luke adds 'When he could not be dissuaded we gave up and said "the Lord's will be done." ' Right words need to be rightly interpreted if they are to be of value to us.

Right interpretations are a crucial element in the exercise of the gift of discernment. One of the best exponents is Joseph. From his experience we can see that a selfless devotion to God is required if we are to receive it (Genesis 41.16). Joseph is gently attentive to the details of Pharaoh's dreams, but knowing he is getting it right he delivers the

word with growing confidence (Genesis 41.82). 'God has
shown Pharaoh what He is about to do.' Most of our problems are caused by an unwillingness to persist in seeking
the Lord after He has first spoken to us. We have to beware
of claiming to know more than the thing He has actually
said to us. To discern accurately requires our attention and
time to wait before him. We need integrity for discernment.
Too often we rest content with an incomplete picture and
a partial word and supplement them by words which come
through the power of our own vivid imagination. Jesus
judged such folly unflatteringly. 'Hypocrites, you know how
to interpret the appearance of the earth and the sky. How
is it that you don't know how to interpret the present time?'
(Luke 12.56).

The Purpose of Discernment in the Body

We should be clear that God does not give us discernment
merely in order to satisfy our own curiosity about another
person's private life. The context for the exercise of the gift
is that of the Gospel of Christ and His salvation, not that
of a church inquisition. To lay claims to possessing great
powers of discernment is a somewhat dubious practice.
When I come across an individual who does this almost
invariably I find that their claim lacks substance. A young
Pastor tells the story of one occasion when he was
approached in this way by a lady in his church. 'I have great
gifts of discernment' she said, 'and so I want to tell you
what's wrong with so and so.' The Pastor's response to this
approach was wise and appropriate. 'You tell me what you
have to say about this person' he said, 'and I will tell you
whether you have great gifts of discernment.' It is sad that
this inner attitude of unkind suspicion is sometimes wrongly
mistaken for the gift of discernment. Such an unchristian
approach always causes much needless hurt and confusion.
On one occasion a young christian couple were victimised
by the missionary group with which they were working and
subjected to a bombardment of charges and accusations all

of which were totally unfounded. They survived all this however, and came to see the truth behind such an experience. For denunciations always say much more about those who make them than they do about their victims. God never gives us the gift of discernment in order to destroy others.

God gives us insight about the needs of others in order to enable us to bring them to the help that they really require. Such was the experience of Barnabas when he visited the young church in Antioch. It had been established through the evangelistic preaching of those who were scattered from Jerusalem following the persecution associated with Stephen's death. When Barnabas arrived there 'he saw the evidence of the grace of God and exhorted them all to remain true to the Lord with all their hearts' (Acts 11.23). Having perceived the grace of God there, he now understood clearly the kind of help that the Church required. This understanding took him on a journey up to Tarsus to find the young man whose conversion had so amazed everybody some years previously. That however, was some time ago and nothing much had been heard of the young man subsequently. His name was Saul, soon to become known as Paul. His ministry was what Antioch required. It was not long before the Church moved out into one of the most exciting new phases of mission recorded in the New Testament. God had granted great discernment to Barnabas and he used it in the positive way that God always intends, to bring the Church of God on. There is no situation that is too insignificant for us to seek and receive discernment for it.

I recall the experience of the wife of one of our dear friends at the very beginning of the fresh moving of the Spirit in Scotland some years ago. The minister Tom Smail our close neighbour, has preaching and teaching gifts which are of exceptional value. In these early days of a fresh touch of the Spirit on our lives we were receiving a lot of helpful ministry from a young Dutch evangelist who frequently visited us in Wishaw. It seemed as if we were all rejoicing in the discovery of new spiritual gifts apart from Tom's wife

Truda. For her it was often an agonising time to share with us because as she did so, she was being constantly reminded of a small incident from her childhood in which she had committed a normal enough transgression affecting her relationship with her sister. Small as the sin was it was nonetheless important to her. She had often remembered it when she went to communion and reflected on the words 'Let a man examine himself and so eat of the bread and drink of the cup.' The memory always had the same effect of plunging her once more into a state of guilty and miserable despair even though the original fault was of little consequence. It only amounted to putting the blame on her sister for picking some flowers in the garden which she was not supposed to touch. This was the situation that the young evangelist Kees unlocked with just a few words: 'Don't you think we ought to speak together about something.' As the need was exposed, so immediately the grace of God's forgiveness, mercy and love was released and she was free. When God grants discernment to us concerning the needs of others including those brought about by their sins which they would sooner keep hidden, it is always to the same end of their forgiveness. Often enough the supposed sins are as trivial as this yet they still leave their mark there. What a relief when we know that they have all gone.

We are also given fresh insights to equip us for spiritual warfare against Satan and his allies. Whilst Christian teachers have freely accepted the reality of the influence of satanic powers in less advanced countries or in earlier ages, nowadays we are needing to face the evidence for their presence much closer to home in our own western society. I have no doubts about the activity and power of evil spirits in our own age, both in the area of our own personal experience and also more significantly within the established structures of the broader institutions of our public life. We will need to take a closer look at the important subject of discernment and the demonic later on. At this point I am only wanting to establish the need for recognising the signs of satanic influence in society at large. Paul discerns the work of the god of this age in the blindness of unbelievers to the light of the Gospel (2 Corinthians 4.4). John sees that all organised-life-without-God in the world is actually under the control of the evil one (1 John 5.19).

It is the same when we see that the cause behind an individual's spiritual problems is in fact demonic. There are almost as many case histories to do with this recorded in the Gospel as there are for the accounts of those whom He physically healed. Discernment is an essential part of our equipment through which we establish the power of the authority of Christ in an area where this has been in dispute.

God enables us to see beneath the outward appearance of a situation in order to open us to His unexpected word. To our orderly western minds the way that God speaks to us does seem strange on occasions. If we have grown up on a good spiritual diet of the daily reading of Scripture following an orderly pattern of reading, the idea of God's Word seizing hold of us in the inward areas of our conscience and spirit may seem to be exceptional. It was not so to a prophet like Jeremiah in the Old Testament. 'His word is in my heart like a burning fire' he exclaims (Jeremiah 20.9). Even an apostate king recognises that the prophet is the man with the word from God's heart. 'Is there any word from the Lord?' asks Zedekiah (37.17) in a private plea to the prophet he has imprisoned. 'Yes', Jeremiah replies, 'you will be handed over to the King of Babylon.' God's word had captured the prophet and he discerns God's purposes accurately from it. The sad confession of all too many Christians is that they seldom hear God speak to them. This is not because the Lord has stopped communicating for even the heavens proclaim His word throughout the whole universe. 'Their voice goes out into all the earth, their words to the end of the world' (Psalm 19.4). God will say plenty of things to those who are prepared to listen to Him.

When the Word of God comes to us in this way there is the sharp sensation of immediate inner recognition as if God was speaking with a voice which is audible. On one occasion for me it was only after a space of several years that I was able to relate together the two parts of one directive word that the Lord had brought to me in this way. The first came when I was awoken one morning by the name of a town in New Zealand ringing in my ear. But the second part was delayed for several years until quite recently I found myself in that city preaching in a large Anglican church in the centre of the town. I was a visitor speaking at a series of conferences at the invitation of David Harper then the Director of Christian Advance Ministries. As I made my way to the church which was packed for the evening meeting I suddenly remembered that strange incident of many years previously. This time the message was clear. 'I am going to show you tonight what that word was all about.' We went on to a meeting that evening in which it seemed to me as if we were nearer to the experience of revival than I have ever been before.

Discernment is a gift which leads to a cultivated sensitivity to the voice of God. How clear and decisive our witness becomes if we have developed the spiritual skills to listen to Him.

Testing Discernment

Gifts of revelation are not sufficient in themselves to bring others into the full life that God makes available to us. It is a great mistake to assume that an accurately spoken word of knowledge will inevitably be followed by the blessing that is needed by those who receive the word. If the insight is accurate we will, however, be in a position to draw the subject a step nearer towards the blessing of God. When Paul receives his famous vision of the man of Macedonia this does not in itself produce the necessary action to bring the Gospel over the Straights of Bosphorus from Asia to Europe. His vision leads to an active step of faith and it is this which God immediately blesses. 'We got ready at once to leave for Macedonia, concluding that God had called us to preach the Gospel to them' (Acts 16.10). To lesser mortals like us it is a very real encouragement to note that

Paul gets his direction right only after a series of setbacks in his plans to travel to Phrygia, Galatia and Bythinia. The seal that Paul and Silas had now got it right soon followed. There are a series of amazing conversions and adventures in Philippi as a result of which a vibrant young Church is established there. We can check out our perceptions by things to which they lead. If they are of God they will lead to the sort of things of which God patently approves. Discernment is granted to the Church so that we might be good stewards of Christ's Gospel and do His work. If they are producing the sad fruits of despondency, fear, division or accusation we may generally assume that our discernment is wrong. If they lead us to faith, hope, love, joy, encouragement and the solution to otherwise intractable problems we can rest secure that we have things right. It is good when we have the eyes that see the reality behind everything that is apparent. It is also important that we have ears to hear too what the Spirit is saying to today's Church.

3

Discernment and Signs and Wonders

God has the power and authority to do whatever He wishes without any further constraint upon Him. Providing the deed is within the scope of His purposes and is consistent with His character, there is nothing beyond the range of His ability. This is what we mean when we describe God as the omnipotent one. He is also omni-present in that He is fully present in different ways and in different places. He is omniscient in that He knows everything, understands everything and recognises everything. Often we have a strange desire to cut God down to the more manageable proportions decreed by our own imagination. All we finish up with is a puny deity made in the mould of man and sustained by his human creator. To follow this humanistic whim is a foolish exercise which is always totally dissatisfying to our spirits and minds. As the nature of God is revealed in Christ He always expands beyond the boundaries of our own intellects. His goodness, holiness and grace balance His awesome majesty. As Paul expresses it in one of his doxologies, 'For from him, through him and to him are all things. To him be glory for ever. Amen' (Romans 11.36).

To share a living relationship with Him is the most amazing privilege available to any of us. The purpose behind Christ's gift of salvation is that we might know this. All the energies of the Holy Spirit are directed to the same end that sharing our life with God, we should come into a knowledge of Him. This knowledge includes but goes beyond an intellectual understanding. It has to do with the persuasion of the heart and the conscience which flows with a living experience. According to the Prophet Daniel, those who have come into this experiential understanding of God are always clearly marked out from others. 'The people who know their God shall stand firm and take action' (Daniel 11.32 RSV). Their understanding stimulates a response which is morally powerful. For although they know that all power belongs to God, they also perceive that He Himself is not dominated by the desire to exercise it. Within the vastness of God Himself there is room for the gentle attributes of kindness, forgiveness and love with which He clothes His power. Nothing is impossible with a God like this nor with those who have come to know Him for themselves.

For this reason the issue of signs and wonders is not new. Inasmuch as they are acts of God through which He demonstrates His powerful grace, they have been around for as long as He has chosen to reveal Himself to us. They were known in the centuries before Christ as one of the ways by which He confirmed His Covenant to Israel. Whenever God intervened in the history of Israel at moments of particular significance, the time was always marked by a flurry of miracles and signs and wonders. We can see this in the account of the escape of the children of Israel from Egypt (Exodus 15.11). Elijah and Elisha's prophetic ministry is similarly attested. Even the pagan King Darius concedes the same point in Daniel's day. 'He is the living God and He endures for ever, His kingdom will not be destroyed, His dominion will never end, He rescues and He saves; He performs signs and wonders in the heaven and on the earth, He has rescued Daniel from the power of the lions' (Daniel 6.16). Their purpose then is the same as it is in the time of Christ. It is that of bringing people into an awareness of the nature of the Lord in order that they might trust in Him and discover His faithfulness for themselves.

Having been clearly demonstrated in these ways over the

centuries prior to Christ, miracles now come into focus in a special way in the ministry of Jesus. They were seen to point to His Messiahship more than His deity. 'We know that you are a teacher come from God. For no one could perform the miraculous signs you are doing if God were not with Him' says Nicodemus to Jesus (John 3.1). Thus they proclaim the inauguration of the long promised kingdom of God which it is the task of the Messiah to introduce. Through the drama of our redemption in Christ's cross, resurrection and ascension they are also released to the Church through the ministry of the Holy Spirit. The function of the Church is always that of being the servant of the Kingdom. Throughout the centuries since they have been known in the history of the Church. Tertullian in the second century speaks about them. Augustine in the fourth century bears testimony to many miracles especially healings and including the raising of the dead. Francis of Assisi in the twelfth century records a vast number of miracles. Healings are also recorded among the early Anabaptists in Europe and the Baptists in England. In the eighteenth century we find John Wesley describing exorcisms, healings and also powerful encounters with the Holy Spirit. In the Pentecostal Movement in the present day we find the attention of Christians returning to this theme which has never totally disappeared from Christian experience. In countries of the Third World in Asia, Africa and South America where the growth of the Church often outstrips the population explosion, there is considerable evidence for present day miracles. Along with an increasing number of others I can testify to the reality of many healings in the course of ordinary pastoral ministry in Inner London. They have seldom happened in a spectacular way. Those who have experienced them are still alive to substantiate the story.

All this being said, we are acutely in need of the gift of discernment when it comes to teaching and testimony about miracles. If a form of Christian rationalism is one profound enemy to true Christian faith, so too is its opposite which is a form of unthinking Charismatic credulity. It is foolish to assume that every claim for a miracle is authentic. Jesus Himself says clearly that there are those who specialise in this area of ministry by relying upon faked claims and unreal testimonies. Good stories can also be unscrupulously used for financial ends. So it is essential for us to use our judgment here, not in order to adopt scepticism but so that we retain our integrity and also some control over our charitable instincts.

Positive Scriptural Teaching

The religion of the Bible is full of signs and wonders. The God of the Bible is one who goes in for miracles of many sorts and in many ways. In the ministry of Jesus four terms are regularly used which take us to the heart of the matter. We need to examine them in order to understand their significance both then and also now in the church of the present day.

The first term is *dunamis* which means *an outward expression of an act of power, of wonder, of miracle or a mighty work*. It is a term which is used some seventy-six times in the New Testament. A typical example in the ministry of Jesus is in Luke 19.37. 'The whole crowd of disciples began joyfully to praise God in loud voices for all the miracles they had seen.' At the same time in Matthew 13.58 we are told that Jesus did not do many of these acts of power in Nazareth because of the atmosphere of sceptical unbelief that prevailed there. On the other hand, in Acts 2.22 we are told that Jesus was a man accredited by God by this means. God actually performed the miracles through Him. In a similar way we are told that King Herod takes a view about the ministry of Jesus which gives another insight into an act of power. He can find no other explanation for Jesus' ministry than the one prompted by his own guilty conscience and supported by the rumours that were then abroad. 'John the Baptist has been raised from the dead and that is why miraculous powers are at work in him' (Mark 6.14). Whilst a miracle operates through the faith of the people involved, in another way it almost seems to operate apart from them. These deeds are done only by means of the Holy Spirit. Though Herod is an evil man he rightly suggests they are acts of power which communicate the very atmosphere of resurrection.

Second *semeion* means a distinguishing mark, an indication, a portent or a sign. It is used some seventy-three times in the New Testament. This term has a most interesting history in the Septuagint, the Greek translation of the Old Testament. There we can see that a sign was never merely an act which illustrates the purpose of God. It has much more prophetic force to it than that. It calls the attention of the people of God to God's action with a view to securing their response. This is the way in which John especially uses it in the New Testament. In his account he records seven great signs in the ministry of Jesus beginning with the changing of the water into wine at the wedding feast of Cana of Galilee. Then in John 20.30 he says that Jesus did many such deeds which are not recorded in the book. He has made a selection of them so that 'you may believe that Jesus is the Christ, the Son of God, and that by believing you may have life in His Name.' The signs of the ministry of Jesus are therefore rather similar to His parables. They can cut both ways. If faith in Christ is there then they feed it. A sign will promote faith and also provoke it. But if there is no such faith even if the signs are multiplied endlessly it is to no avail. Even though they may present an effective revelation of His salvation with regard to healing, the spectators will not profit by them. Faith in Christ is always the ultimate purpose and signs may be a means to that end if they are properly received and interpreted. But faith is never an automatic response which can be triggered off by a few spectacular acts. In John 12.37 we are told that though the people had seen many signs they still would not believe in Him, for there is no such thing as unwilling faith.

Thirdly, the term *ergon* (literally, 'work') means a deed or a manifestation or a practical proof. It is used eighteen times in the New Testament, and when used to describe the acts of men refers to the deeds which exhibit a consistent moral character which may be either good or bad. The deeds of Jesus are consistently wonderful in that they are a practical proof of his relationship with the Father. In John 5.17 Jesus said: 'My Father is always at his work to this very day and I too am working.' What is perhaps even more surprising is that He promises that we will do the same deeds ourselves and even greater ones. 'I tell you the truth, anyone who has faith in me, will do what I have been doing. He will do even greater things than these because I am going to the Father' (John 14.12). They are a practical demonstration of the same kind of relationship for ourselves. These deeds are given to the Son as He gives Himself to the Father's mission. They are given to the Church likewise as we are obedient to the task He has appointed. A disobedient Church will be interested only in signs and wonders as means by which they can bolster up their own flagging insecurity. But they will never receive them. It is to the Church which is willing to do the Father's bidding that they become more immediately available.

Lastly, *teras* is used consistently with semeion and means a wonder. It describes the psychological effect of many signs in that they create an atmosphere in which true faith in the living God is substantiated. In Acts 3.10 the miraculous event has taken place and a man who has been lame from birth is now walking, leaping and praising God. Since it all defies rational explanation we are told that they were all filled with wonder and amazement at what had happened. They could not understand it but they could not get away from it. The exceptional deed points to an extraordinary Lord and it is at this point that Peter goes on to speak about Him. As is always the case in the Scriptures, those who witness the event are not left merely to ponder on these things. As Peter speaks about Jesus He and John have their first experience of a hostile reaction, but the more important result is of a very different kind. 'Many who heard the message believed, and the number of men grew to about 5,000' (Acts 4.4).

Now all these terms are employed to describe a wide range of activities inspired by God. There are many case histories in the Gospels describing straightforward healings which are miracles. There are also miracles which are truly extraordinary. These include healings which take place at a distance without even the touch of Jesus or His presence. There are three instances of resuscitations. In the village of Nain, Luke 7.11 Jesus interrupts a funeral procession to restore a son to his widowed mother. In Luke 8.41 a little girl of twelve years of age is restored to life shortly after her death. In John 11.1 we are told of the most famous incident of all. Lazarus who is a friend of Jesus and brother to Mary and Martha is sick and dies. Four days after his death Jesus comes and restores him, even though by this time his body must have been in a state of decay.

In addition to this there are the miracles in nature like the miracle recorded in all four Gospels of the great multiplication of food and fish for a crowd of at least 5,000. There are numerous accounts of sudden conversions to Christ, always the greatest miracle for the convert and the most astonishing sign to those who witness it. There are miracles of exorcism and miracles of judgment when the power of God falls upon those who are perpetrating fearful acts. We will need to look in closer detail at some of these later on. At this point we simply notice that signs and wonders are never deeds which stand on their own without interpretation. They are always a means by which the Gospel message of Christ is clarified and His claims presented. As we discover their significance for the Church today we need to summarise how they relate to the Gospel.

Firstly, signs and wonders often anticipate a presentation of the Gospel message to stir up interest. This is the case in the incident just referred to in Acts 3 and 4. It is not that the healing miracle is an unusual event in itself but that it opens the door for effective evangelism. There is no other explanation for it than this. It is an act of intervention on the part of a loving Lord towards a world which is desperately in need of Him. Peter goes on to make this clear by his strong preaching of the basic message or kerygma to which we must always return.

Secondly, signs and wonders often accompany the preaching of the Gospel. Jesus followed this word and deed method in His own ministry. So also did Paul. 'I will not venture to speak of anything except what Christ has accomplished through me in leading the Gentiles to obey God by what I have said and done, by the power of signs and miracles through the power of the Holy Spirit. So from Jerusalem all the way round to Illyricum I have fully proclaimed the Gospel of Christ' (Romans 15.18–19). His presentation was directed to the mind and conscience of his hearer as ours must be also. But this was not done in a matter that was exclusive of the factual and practical evidence. There were signs and wonders to be taken into account, also all of which point to one conclusion. It is that of the necessity of a sound and saving faith in Christ.

Thirdly, signs and wonders may also be said to authenticate the Gospel message. They give examples of God's grace to the needy people who must receive it. We are given numerous accounts of ways in which miracles follow his own deep inner heart stirring. The Greek verb *splagchnizomai* describes this. It refers to an emotion which reaches into the inward parts, or the bowels or the entrails. It describes what we would call a gut reaction to a situation. This was how Jesus felt in Nain when He saw the funeral procession (Luke 7.13). Perhaps we could say that it is not just that Jesus would not leave the situation alone but that He could not. Mercy, grace, love and kindness revolted at the thought. Thus He gave proof of His generous character as the Son of the God who is revealed in the Gospel.

Fourthly, signs and wonders activate a definite response to the Gospel. Having set the appropriate framework of God in Christ redeeming the world out of His loving mercy they may promote a robust faith in Him as a consequence. It is interesting to note that nearly two-thirds of the references to faith in the first three Gospels occur in relation to miracles. Not that miracles always secure this response.

They may produce an opposite result, but at least it will be clear. Miracles are like the electric light switch. When they happen, the power circuit is complete, the light comes on and darkness is dispelled. They are powerful inducements to faith in Christ. More people are likely to come to faith by this means than by others. A secular Church is such a dull institution but they can waken the Church up to its full potential as God's witness. We need to learn about miracles so that we can see their relevance. Even if they occur less frequently then some would be prepared to acknowledge for reasons which we are about to discuss, they do still happen today.

Limitations to Miracles

Having outlined a case for the inclusion of signs and wonders as important evidence for the presence of the Kingdom of God today there are some further strands of teaching from the Scripture which we need to consider. They carry another part of the message to us. As always we need to return to the heart of the message of the Gospel which is the *Good News of Jesus Himself. There is no alternative sign or wonder for the world today than* that of Christ Himself. Indeed, Christ incarnate in the person of the infant babe is 'the sign that will be spoken against' as the ancient Simeon declared to Mary His mother (Luke 2.34). Christ risen from the dead, the sign of the prophet Jonah (Luke 11.29) is the one sign that the miraclemongering masses in the days of Christ would not tolerate. If we have all sorts of signs, wonders and phenomena and yet somehow have lost sight of Him in His life, death, resurrection, ascension and coming then in the end of the day we have nothing to offer. He is the sign and it is only inasmuch as miracles point to Him that they have worth. The sound, sense and substance of the Gospel is Christ, always infinitely more glorious than any deed by which His power may be made known. Since there are no alternatives it follows that signs and wonders must never be used as a substitute message to the Gospel. The message of the Apostles was that of the cross and resurrection (Galatians 6.14). The greatest glory of the cross is that it is God's chosen method by which He atones for us for our sins in His suffering love and obtains our forgiveness. There is a clear connection between our sins and our sicknesses as there is also between His suffering and our healing. We will explore this further but we must insist that the message which we preach has to do with sins more than headaches, guilt and forgiveness more than rheumatism. In short it is cross centred and so it must remain. Scripture indicates the reason for this emphasis. For the fact is that whilst there is a real place for miracles *the modern phenomena associated with them may not necessarily be Christian but may indeed be specifically non-Christian*. This is always so when too much significance is claimed for events which in themselves may be very trivial such as the so-called experience of resting in the Spirit or being slain in the Spirit. On occasions this can be a beautiful time of encounter with our healing Lord. It may indeed mark a time of spiritual conflict as is suggested in 1 Corinthians 14.25. However, it may just be a conditioned response to the preacher's unspoken request for a sign and wonder. We have to assess these things by the ways in which they occur and their effective value. This is even more necessary when the manifestation is blatantly artificial, the product of a deliberate attempt to deceive the unwary. Jesus warns us of this precise danger. Many will have laid claims to great skills in prophecy, exorcism or miracle working He says, but His word to them at the last day will be 'I never knew you' (Matthew 7.22). The so-called miracle will have been an evil deed performed by an evil person. He goes on to point out that spiritual charlatans who specialise in great Charismatic ministries will be a feature of the end days (Mark 13.22). Jesus Himself puts a limitation in the value of signs and wonders and in John 4:48 he complains 'Unless you people see miraculous signs and wonders you will not believe.' After the resurrection He tells His disciples that it is more blessed to believe even if we have not had the aid of a mighty miracle (John 20.29).

Paul agrees with this and indicates that miracles, signs and wonders will certainly be in the repertoire of the ultimate man of sin who will finally emerge (2 Thessalonians 2.9).

As soon as modern miracle workers adopt the aura of omniscience so that they cannot be challenged or corrected by their peers we must be extremely cautious. If great significance is attached to the deed or its execution so that little attention is focused on the Lord Himself it is likely to be altogether false. Signs and wonders never override the terms or aims of the Gospel. The purpose of the Gospel is to bring rebellious man into obedience to God (Romans 15.8). God's mercies are offered to us in Christ in order to stimulate an unreserved offering of ourselves to God (Romans 12.1–2). We need to remain mentally and spiritually alert whenever the signs and wonder issue is being discussed lest these goals be abandoned for others which are far less worthy, although for some far more intriguing.

I doubt whether the Lord will entrust the modern Church in the western world with very much more in signs and wonders unless we develop a higher degree of integrity. *The problem at the root of many claims for signs and wonders is a lack of discernment.* Jesus always screened these things very carefully and so must we. It is because of my positive faith in both their reality and their value that I urge a far greater degree of stringency than we have shown thus far. All too often an understandable desire to see miracles today overcomes our critical faculties. If we are not careful we find ourselves defending healings as great miracles before they have been tested out at all. The consequence can be both sad and disillusioning both for the person who has received the ministry and also for those who have given it. Kathryn Kuhlman was the well-known preacher with an astonishing healing ministry which lasted for over 50 years. In her biography by Jamie Buckingham, *Daughter of Destiny*, we are told of the rules she always applied before a healing could be written about in one of her books.

a) The disease or injury should be organic or structural in nature and should have been medically diagnosed.

b) The healing should have occurred rapidly or instantaneously. The changes would have to be abnormal and not the kind that could result from suggestion.

c) All healings would have to be medically verified, preferably by more than one doctor. At least one of the doctors must be the patient's private physician.

d) The healing should be permanent or at least of sufficient duration so as not to be diagnosed as a remission.

All of these rules are still relevant for us today. In the time of Jesus it was the priest who would know whether a leprosy sufferer was sick or healed. Jesus' words to the ten sufferers was 'Go, show yourself to the priest' (Luke 17.14). 'As they went they were cleansed', Luke adds. A public testing and affirmation was essential however, and it still is today if the consequences of the healing are likely to affect the lives of others.

Practical Guidelines

Having insisted upon the possibility of miracles and yet indicated some of the dangers of that view, we come to the criteria which discerning Christians should look out for.

Firstly, Christ Himself is the sign, the wonder, the act of power and the miracle. The priority question therefore must always be about Him. What does the event say of Him? Does it point us to Him? Does it lead us to glorify Him more and obey Him more? 'All the prophets testify about Him' says Peter (Acts 10.43). If there is the slightest suggestion of a compromise at this point then whatever the deed we do well to reject it. Yet such is His grace towards His people that He frequently demonstrates His love in healing, even when they have only known Him for a short while.

Secondly, the foundation for faith in the possibility of miracles is that this is the teaching of the Bible. We ground our faith not on amazing testimonies or powerful ministries but on the Scriptures. The God of the Bible can work a miracle any time He likes and by any means. We must add that along with miracles the human manifestations that accompany them that are described in the Bible are quite enough for us to be going along with. Non-Biblical manifestations may be highly sensational but they are also very suspect. When healers speak about fields of power, strange auras, fluttering eyelids, trembling, hot hands and also swooning it is wise to remain somewhat sceptical. All of these things may be observable, but to what end? I suspect that they may well be a response to suggestion. One rather funny variant on the same theme is to do with the vibrating hands of those who minister, as if they have been plugged into a power driven massage machine. It means nothing at all. There are very many more who have been healed without any of these accompanying experiences. We should be as careful with them as the Scriptures are. Unless there is a clear Scriptural mandate discreet silence is the golden rule.

Thirdly, all God given experiences are self authenticating. If a word about healing is from God, a person is healed without further exhortations. We can see this frequently in Scripture. It cannot be attributed totally to their great faith for often that is of a very low order. Similarly, if God speaks a calming word to a troubled person they become astonishingly peaceful. If it is a liberating word they may well be gloriously, even hilariously, released. When God acts it is obvious and wonderful.

Lastly, the Scriptural context for signs and wonders is most frequently mission. In the Gospels Jesus does not hold secret seminars on healing hidden in the hills of Galilee. They have a crash course on the job. Having shown them how He ministered, He sends forth the twelve (Luke 9.1). Shortly after this He commissions the seventy-two (Luke 10.1). The whole Church is soon engaged in the same ministry. We can see from the book of Acts it is that of making Christ known to others who are lost without Him. I do not believe that God grants miracles to a church which is either self-seeking or self-centred. The idea that we can learn a bit about these things in a cosy atmosphere before we take on the mission outside is suspect on Scriptural grounds. This suggestion all too easily panders to the self centred desire of those for whose whole Christian experience is need based rather than founded on God. But when the disciples dare to obey they are thrilled at the results. 'The seventy-two returned with joy and said "Lord, even the demons submit to us in your Name" ' (Luke 10.17). Signs and wonders are the means by which non-Christians are stirred to faith in Christ. I believe that the next major renewal contribution to the whole Church is here at this point. As God has used the renewal to stimulate and transform our worship, so He will use fresh insights into miracles to transform our mission, providing we maintain intregrity over our claims. The Holy Spirit puts the spotlight on Jesus in this way. They are relevant especially for those whose sight has been dazzled by other illuminations.

Using God given insight and the capacity to weigh things carefully we can see that their ultimate purpose then is not that of providing some spectacular relief for Christians when their spirits are low. Rather they are given in order to prompt faith in a God who can grant them and withhold them at will. Our confidence is based on His character. He will not always heal the sick in body, mind and spirit (in the next chapter we will look at this more closely) but He will always come when we call – in sickness or in health.

4

Discernment and Healing

My first attempt at a healing ministry ended in abject failure. The sick lady died only two weeks after I had prayed for her. Not that I had called to minister full of confident faith in the power of Christians to heal in Christ's Name today. I had come to this view somewhat reluctantly, it was the lady herself who did the rest. She had read her Bible and arrived at the conclusion that Jesus specialised in this kind of thing. She knew also that she was desperately sick with cancer and so was prepared to take any chance that was on offer – even through a young and inexperienced minister. Her death was a great sadness for the family. For me there was an added sense of personal disappointment too. I had stepped out in obedience to God's command to heal the sick and He had still let her die. Yet there was one factor that was really intriguing. For her last two weeks she had never needed any more pain killing drugs. Whether or not I understood it, this made me see that there was something about praying for sick people in the Name of Jesus that was powerful in itself. It suggested that maybe there was sufficient to learn in this area of ministry to open up a whole new range of possibilities if only it could be pursued with care.

Since that time I must have ministered to many dozens of sick people and witnessed many astonishing healings among people of all ages and backgrounds. My own wife is in their number. Yet I would be lacking in integrity if I gave the impression that it is always unambiguously effective. This is not so. There is probably more enigma attached to the healing ministry of the Church today than to any other part of the work. Even if we adopt the position more easily held by itinerant preachers than resident pastors that all that we need is the faith to believe for healing, it still remains problematic. Some are healed but many are not. For some it is just a temporary remission. For others despite intense prayer and every kind of ministry sickness often continues along its expected course. Hence the ministry as a whole remains perplexing. Whenever we fail to exercise discernment it can become one that is shrouded with myth that easily turns to guilt or even dangerous deception. Yet it all remains potentially so promising. Who can measure the blessing of one person unexpectedly restored to fulness of health after a period of illness? If our prayers have had some part in this, who can resist the opportunity of trying? So we need to make a start, using all the tools of intelligent perception in the process. That means the need to think the healing issue through carefully, scripturally and accurately.

To begin, it is useful to establish a Christian attitude to the medical profession. My own understanding is that we should always be constructive in our relationship with those who deal with sickness and disease with the advantage of professional expertise whether or not they happen to believe. I have never seen any good in the view that there is a clash of interests here. I have often seen great harm from those who take that view and one example will suffice. We have only ever suffered from a small number of defections to new churches from our own home church in Streatham where I ministered formerly. One of the saddest was quite recent. A small group left the church to join a small new fellowship committed to the 'restoration' pattern of churchmanship. Unfortunately the preacher in the new church became seriously ill with pneumonia and other associated chest complaints although he was quite a young man. Despite this he insisted on leading a church holiday away from home in bitterly cold weather. He was assured

that all was well for him and that there was no need for the
treatment any competent GP would have prescribed. Whilst
he was away the pneumonia developed rapidly and he died.
Even this sad event did not shake the confidence of his
flock on the adequacy of prayer and faith without outside
professional help. It was only fours days after his death that
his zealous group decided that he was not, after all, to be
restored to life in their midst, and that therefore they should
inform the outside world. We can well imagine what a
devastating experience this must have been, but what about
its wider impact on society as a whole? And there were
even worse consequences. In their desire to find a cause for
their failure they turned upon the late pastor's wife who
was heavily pregnant at the time. It was all due to her lack
of faith. So in addition to the task of bringing a child into
the world without the assurance of her husband by her side,
she was now the scapegoat burdened with the responsibility
for his death too. How unkind and dangerous such teaching
as this is. Not surprisingly it destroyed the little fellowship
they had gathered.

I insist that none of this need have happened with a
Christian approach to medical treatment. For us it is never
either/or but always both/and. Christians who are laymen
in medical affairs should not presume to give clinical advice
for which they do not hold the appropriate qualifications.
If the sick person has been on a course of medication then
let those who prescribed it bring it to an end. They will be
willing enough to do so if the malady that caused the trouble
has manifestly cleared. Whenever someone is healed of
anything of a serious nature or with any kind of social
consequence for the lives of others, I urge them to seek
confirmation for their healing from those who are best able
to give it. The Scriptures accept the place of knowledge
gained by scientific study. Common sense enlightened by
the Holy Spirit confirm this. There is no healing ministry
being conducted by anyone anywhere in the world today
which can afford to avoid these obvious needs.

Healing's Scriptural Foundations

As the Gospels describe the life and ministry of Jesus, we are immediately impressed by the quantity of the references to healing that they contain. Someone has computed that 727 verses out of a total of 3,729 are devoted to this theme. It means that allowing for all the narrative describing both Christ's birth and His betrayal, trial, death, and resurrection and all His parables, nonetheless approximately one verse in five describes a healing. There are over forty case histories recorded in some detail as we shall see. The clear message that all this communicates is not that of the evangelical paradigm. This is the view that healings demonstrate the grace of forgiveness since sickness is a picture of sin. It is that Christ has come to heal the sick because He sees sickness for what it is. It is an offence against the image of God in man, and an ultimate byproduct of humanity's lostness. So the Sun of Righteousness has arisen in Jesus. There is healing in His wings for us.

The first grounds for our expectation for healing are laid in a broad understanding of what it was that Jesus came both to teach and to do. The word which summarises His ministry and message is *salvation*. As Son of God and Saviour He has come to announce the news that salvation has come in Him. This is the significance of His Name. 'You are to give him the name Jesus because he will save his people from their sins' (Matthew 1.21). It is also the opening theme of Mary's beautiful response to her own pregnancy. 'My soul praises the Lord and my spirit rejoices in God my Saviour' (Luke 1.47).

Salvation carries four meanings. *Firstly, wholeness or ultimate perfection*. It speaks of 'that which saves a man from all that would ruin his soul in this life and in the life to come' (William Barclay). Paul assures the believers in Philippi of this ultimate result. 'They (your opponents) will be destroyed, but you will be saved and that by the grace of God' (Philippians 1.28). We enter salvation now and are at present enjoying its benefits, but its full impact awaits the completion of God's purposes in Christ's return and final triumph.

Secondly, salvation means deliverance and protection. Ancient Israel rejoiced in this in the Exodus experience from Egypt. As they gathered by the banks of the Red Sea, hemmed in by their enemies Moses said: 'Do not be afraid, stand firm and you will see the *deliverance* the Lord will bring to you today . . . The Lord will fight for you' (Exodus 14.13). From their place of safety on the other side of the sea they burst into a song which is recorded in the Old Testament and then repeated in the New: 'The Lord is my strength and my song; he has become my salvation, he is my God' (Exodus 15.2; Revelation 15.3).

Thirdly, salvation speaks of forgiveness from sin and all human lostness. Christ's coming was to this end (Matthew 1.21). He sought and saved that which was lost (Matthew 18.11; Luke 19.10). He sends sin and guilt packing because of the cross and through His grace (Ephesians 2.5; 1 Corinthians 1.18). He requires our repentance and faith in Himself as a consequence (Ephesians 2.8; 2 Corinthians 7.10).

Lastly, salvation also refers to the physical healing of our bodies. In one story in the Gospels a sinful woman is forgiven and saved through faith (Luke 7.50). In the next chapter it is a sick woman with a haemmorrhagic condition who is received and healed through faith (Luke 8.48). Salvation relates to both conditions and the terms used are actually identical. The Church today is beginning to awaken to the breadth of this ministry and also to the relevance of its application. For every saving experience is an anticipation of all that is yet to come at the last. It may be in the form of deliverance, forgiveness or healing but it is an intrusion of the future into the present, since the Saviour is always the Lord of both time dimensions. Indeed, He looks after our past as well.

Another fundamental for healing is that it is plainly an important part of Christ's teaching on the *theme of the Kingdom of God*. This Kingdom is the overwhelming emphasis of His ministry and forms a convenient metaphor by which we may summarise His message. As to its meaning, the Kingdom speaks of God's dynamic rule inaugurated in Jesus. It was anticipated and specifically promised in the Old Testament but now in Jesus it has come (Matthew 3.2; 4.17; 4.32). Whenever the king is present, there we find the kingdom.

The relevance of this is in the light of an underlying assumption. Christ's teaching on His Kingdom is to be set over against His understanding of two kingdoms. His is the rule of light, joy and righteousness but the other is one of darkness, gloom and despair (Colossians 1.12–13). Moreover, in Jesus, God is re-establishing His rule in the world He has made but which has been hi-jacked by a usurper, the devil. Hence, whenever God's Kingdom comes it challenges the rule of an alien intruder. There is an inevitable conflict and plenty of evidence of the clash (Mark 1.23; Matthew 4.1; 1 John 5.19).

In order to enter God's kingly rule it is necessary for us to repent and believe the Good News (Matthew 4.17). This will involve the inward conversion of our spirits as we become like little children in our approach to God our Father (Matthew 18.3). John puts this in a different way by using the language of regeneration. 'I tell you the truth, unless a man is born again he cannot see the Kingdom of God' (John 3.3). Naturally speaking, Jesus insists we neither desire the rule of God nor are we qualified to enter it. It is only possible by the most radical change initiated by the action of the Holy Spirit within us.

Healings are an outward sign of the presence and reality of the Kingdom of God, as Jesus reminds John the Baptist at his time of great personal despondency (Luke 7.21 ff). Yet it has not come in its fulness at this time. Like salvation, it also has a future dimension to it which is not yet seen (Matthew 24.14; 25.1; 1 Corinthians 15.50). Healings demonstrate the power and authority of Christ's rule over the activities of both the devil and disease. In the ministry of Jesus subsequently, they also show how death must yield to His lordly rule (Luke 9.1). They speak of a reign which has already been established in His coming and by His cross. But the fact is that His Kingdom still remains a future event even though it is present now. It is here that we find the chief explanation as to why it is that our present ministry of healing always remains an adventure of faith. Healings demonstrate the final events of the reign of Christ which is not yet seen. They project us forward to that glad day when Christ's return establishes His final reign. Yet that day still remains ahead of us, and so too do some of our healings. If we ignore this future factor for healing it may well be the case that the ministry of healing produces more baffling problems than it solves.

On these twin foundations of a present salvation and of the kingdom awaiting its consummation we may build a sound practice of healing today. To neglect the kingdom altogether and to concentrate only on a message of salvation from inward sin is to spiritualise God's wholistic grace. It is people that God is concerned with, nor merely disembodied spirits. To obscure the fact that the Kingdom in its fulness is not yet come, is to open the door to charismatic miracle mongering that will be bound at least to disappoint because its theology is defective. So we will find ourselves surrounded either by the accusers or the experts. Both are roaming the ranges of church life these days. They build their teachings from some of their experiences, zealously conserving the good stories, always omitting those that do not fit. In the first group are those who explain sickness and even the inconvenient death of one to whom they have ministered often in terms of the unbelief of the sufferer. It is a cruel message, only compounding the weight of personal pain to the individual concerned. It is unconvincing since in the end of the day God is both the author and giver of faith (Hebrews 12.1; Ephesians 2.8). I remain highly sceptical of the methods and the motives of those who claim to do more than a broad Biblical understanding would ever allow. In the second category are those who are not accusing but are always instructing. 'We do not heal today because we do not know how.' They say that with a certain degree of truth. They then embark on the courses to teach all on the assumption that we will sooner or later know all and heal all and thus establish the rule of God in our midst. Yet they omit a serious theological reflection on the common experience of failure. They do not allow much for the reality of suffering as an element of discipleship. They suggest that God no longer has the option to use it, that He so plainly manifested both in the experience of Jesus and Paul (Matthew 27.45; 2 Corinthians 12.7). They omit the teaching that speaks of our present experience necessarily involving the suffering and pressures which are still on a creation spoiled by sin (Romans 8.18). Moreover, they think that to talk success is to produce it. But God grants spontaneous healings as He wishes and not on demand. We need to find another foundation for ministry rather than this one, for the purpose of our ministry should always be to communicate the grace of God whether a person is physically healed in the end or whether they are not. We do not wish to cause added frustration and hurt by the teaching which we give.

The best scriptural base for an effective healing ministry is that of a local church in which Christ's compassionate love is plainly seen and felt. Set the task of healing on the agenda of normal ministry, alongside worship, teaching, mission and the practical service of the church and it is safely located. Practice it within the regular pattern of sacrament, prayer and fellowship and it will be a blessing both to those who receive it and to those who minister. It is a church which knows plenty of healing for itself which can minister plenty of healing to others. We look for churches where love abounds with such joy and spontaneous caring that everyone is blessed by the opportunity of extending healing grace. It is always possible to enter into healing in such an environment. For to fail or even to die is no longer a disgrace. The dignity of the sick believer and those who minister is preserved by the abundance of love.

We have seen many healings in Streatham. Hydro-cephalus, Hirchsprung's disease, ulcerative colitis, cancer and Khrone's disease are all on the list of those who received healing in the past together with the usual additions of healing to the limbs, the pelvis, headaches and all the rest. One of our most notable successes was actually in the death of our first fulltime lady worker, Connie Norton. This may seem a perverse example to cite in support of a healing ministry, so let me go on to explain. Connie was a thoroughly convinced advocate of the possibility of healing and was as eager as anyone to engage in the ministry. When her own sickness was diagnosed this made her reaction all the more significant. 'Wonderful', she said, 'that means I will soon be with Jesus.' We resisted this conclusion and insisted on ministering to her for healing until the Lord brought an unmistakeable message confirming her word through the lips of one of the church's rough diamonds, a recently converted released and transformed ex-homosexual who is still in the church to this day. 'Yes, her work is finished', he announced to the Church gathered for a half night of prayer on the matter. 'You must let her go', he concluded. It took us about thirty minutes to digest that declaration and to react to it with unanimous agreement that it was exactly what we already knew in our hearts. The consequence was that the half night of prayer came to a swift end and we retired home to our beds earlier than we had expected. From that time on I prepared Connie as best I could for the journey ahead for her. Outwardly she wasted away but inwardly she was renewed day by day. When she was ready for the eternal glory that far outweighs all else I kept my last promise. It meant a desperate dash home from a conference but I made it in time to say, 'Connie, I've come to see you off. It's time for you to go now.' Within ten minutes she left her sister Hilda and me behind by her bedside and slipped silently into heaven.

It is a shame when those who are sick travel far and wide for healing ministry since their own church is not prepared to embark on it. At all costs we must endeavour to spare many of them that desolate journey home from the euphoric atmosphere of a large conference where so much has been said about healing and yet so little has happened. We can make a beginning at least by committing ourselves to healing just among the people where we are in the ordinary ongoing life of ordinary low key churches.

Patterns For Ministry

From the chart on page 57 we can see that scriptural healing affects sickness at four different levels. Organic sickness has to do with the malfunction of an organ or a physical part of the body. There are also many forms of illness associated with the presence and the activity of demons as the references show. We will open up this subject in the next chapter. The section headed neurotic and psychological disease would undoubtedly need to be expanded in the light of our present day knowledge of the psychosomatic factor. Nevertheless, it is interesting to note how Jesus indicated a source of sickness here in one of the stress factors of modern society. It is through anxiety for which He prescribes the cure in terms of faith in Himself. There is then the section on resuscitations and the healings of an unspecified kind generally affecting large numbers of people with various maladies, all of whom are healed simultaneously.

Jesus uses a variety of methods in His healing. Touch was clearly important for Him (Matthew 8.15). It is a means of communication between us which has more significance than we have often realised. He uses prayer to His Father linked with a positive command to the sick, or in the case of Lazarus to the dead (John 11.41). Often He directs a straight command to the sick person to do what their sickness says they can't. 'Get up' to a paralysed man (Luke 5.17). 'Stretch out your hand' to someone who had a withered arm (Luke 6.10). 'Be opened' He says to the blocked ears and the locked tongue of a deaf and dumb man (Mark 7.34–35). He allowed others to touch Him and healing power flowed forth (Luke 8.42). He mixed saliva and mud and used it to anoint the eyes of the blind (Mark 7.31). He sanctioned the use of oil for anointing the sick (Mark 6.13). He also repeated a ministry more than once in the case of the man whose sight was partially restored and then later became fully clear (Mark 8.22). Faith was also clearly an important element. When it was conspicuous by its absence as in Nazareth, nothing much happened (Mark 6.5). When faith was present, albeit of a vicarious kind being exercised for the sick person rather than by them, anything seemed likely, certainly healing. Sometimes He healed at a distance without ever coming into the presence of the sick person (Luke 7.10).

From Christ's methodology in healing there are three important applications for our own healing today. *Firstly the variety of His approach* is in sharp contrast with the stereotyped way in which we often work. I suspect that He chose different methods for the very good reason that disease and sickness is itself always with complications. We should become a great deal more flexible than we are if we are to find what is appropriate in the case of each individual who is before us.

Secondly He recognises that while sickness may be biological in its origin due to microbes which carry disease and enter the system, it may be due to demonic factors or through sin and guilt (Luke 5.20; 8.2). In the Gospels as it is today, demons tend to make their presence felt as we shall see later on. But the sin factor is more difficult to detect, requiring sure and steady discernment without heartless accusation. In a case of paralysis it was clearly a main factor. But in the case of blindness it was equally plainly irrelevant (John 9.2). Accuracy with our understanding will not lead us into hasty condemnations of the sick person but into strong and effective ministry which will make them well.

Thirdly, having noted the place of faith in His ministry, we land ourselves in great difficulty if we turn faith into demand or even more, into accusation. The answer to little faith is much Scripture (Romans 10.17). We need to feed on the word which will itself produce faith. It doesn't happen in a mechanical way. It happens by giving us a God dimension to our thinking. More than that, faith is a gift (Ephesians 2.8) and one especially associated with the healing gifts. Paul pairs the two of them together (1 Corinthians 12.9). It is better to go to God for faith than to swallow all the triumphalistic stories under the sun. For God will give it in the measure in which we ask for it and for which it is suitable. Then it will grow as we exercise it in a godly way. You will always know when you are edging away from faith into fantasy by the disturbing sense which begins to grip you inwardly. I confess that I have known that troubling experience on a few occasions when I have wandered away from God, like a foolish rebellious son. My advice is, do not do it. You will only have to make your own way home in due course, chastened by the sad experiences which have accompanied your escapades. We stay in safety when we exercise our faith to the full and show this by staying close to the Father who gives it.

Resolving The Healing Enigma

Having looked at the grounds for a healing ministry in the Church today and having also examined some of the ways in which we can do it, I think it is necessary to set down the factors which will enable us to engage in the practice with sensitivity and integrity. Jesus said that He only did what He saw the Father doing and that without this understanding He could do nothing at all (John 5.19). It is the same for us too. It is certain that we *cannot pretend* to do what God is not doing. Certainly He is not dissembling, exaggerating or lying in order to establish a base for ministry and no more should we. It does not come about merely on the grounds of our expectancy but on the grounds of God's grace.

Moreover, the Lord still speaks to His people today. The first step towards exercising an effective healing ministry is that of hearing what He is saying concerning the one for whom we pray and ministering to them accordingly. If we do not pick up anything at all from Him the fault may well

be with us. It may be the case however, that neither the
time nor the occasion is appropriate for anything more than
a prayer of blessing and that the important moments are
yet to come. Hence we should minister only a prayer of
blessing on such an occasion – asking the Lord to fulfil all
that He desires in His own time and way.

Jesus makes it clear that our healing is through His
suffering and uses the figure of Isaiah the suffering servant
to make this clear (Matthew 8.17). There is a link between
His cross and our healing, but suffering is also a means of
God's glory. 'This was to fulfil what was spoken through
the prophet Isaiah, He took up our infirmities and carried
our diseases.' It always seems wise to me to note that whilst
we may rightly regard healing as being God's normal
purpose, on occasions He is working to a different end.
Sickness may be an option He wants to take up to teach us
lessons of grace that we would not otherwise learn. This
was certainly Paul's experience (2 Corinthians 12.7). It is
little more than special pleading to say that this passage
teaches otherwise. The messenger of Satan is a thorn in
Paul's flesh and not his spirit. Yet it is also the means by
which he learns 'My grace is sufficient for you and my
strength is made perfect in your physical weakness.'

So it will remain the case for those who engage in this
ministry with the firmest convictions and the greatest
charism. We will always have a sufficient experience of
God's healing grace to know that His salvation is present.
We will not have a totality of it however, since His Kingdom
is not yet come in its fulness. Healings are events of grace
in the inbetween times until the day of God dawns. As with
sickness so also with death. Travel to Israel today as often as
you can afford to but you will never meet Lazarus, Tabitha,
Eutychus, Jairus' daughter or the widow's son in Nain.
Having died once and been resuscitated they lived again for
a period then death claimed them again. The truly unique
part of their experience is that they are those who have
tasted death twice, whereas for the rest of us it is a once
only experience. It is also with those nameless holy ones

who travelled around after the death and resurrection of Jesus, presumably to be consigned to fresh tombs the second time round (Matthew 27.52–53). There have been the occasional stories of other resuscitations through to this present day. The ministry of Pastor William Duma in South Africa is a modern example, yet we are still under the rule of death even though we genuinely believe in Christ and look for healing. 'He who believes in me will live even though he dies and whoever lives and believes in me will never die', says Jesus (John 11.25–26).

Moreover, death comes to the believer in Christ as a friend and never a foe whatever form it takes. 'For me to live is Christ and to die is gain', declares Paul (Philippians 1.21). A satisfactory assurance of this will rob the enemy of a powerful tool against us in our time of physical weakness near our end. It will also protect the healing ministry from one of its most macabre distortions. The suggestion that the devil's power is such that he can more or less pick us off and kill us as he wishes if we are on his hit list, is an appalling distortion of what Scripture plainly teaches. 'If God be for us who can be against us? He who did not spare His own Son but gave Him up for us all, how will He not also with Him graciously give us all things . . . Now in all these things we are more than conquerors . . . over death, life, angels, demons . . . Nothing will be able to separate us from the love of God that is in Christ Jesus our Lord' (Romans 8.31). Far from death being the enemy's trump card it is always in the hands of Jesus declares John. 'I have the keys of death and hades', says the risen Lord in John's vision (Revelation 1.18). To suggest anything other than this is defective theology with appalling pastoral consequences. In short no Church can engage in a satisfactory healing ministry without an adequate Christian doctrine of suffering and also of death conquered in Christ.

Within these limits the last factor to mention is to do with the ongoing work of the Holy Spirit with us through which we may be equipped for healing action. It is significant that Jesus never began to minister healing until He was consciously endued with the Holy Spirit and His power. Yet once this had happened He seldom seemed to stop (see Luke 3.22; 4.1; 4.14; 4.36,38). With the anointing of the Holy Spirit there also came the directing of the Holy Spirit with all the discerning gifts that are necessary for effective ministry. The chief cause for complaint for those who claim too much for their healing ministry is just the same as it is for those who never even attempt it at all. In both cases they fail because they lack insight into what is really needed and what God is really doing. This shortage of discernment highlights the greatest lack for a healing Church. How sad it is if its substitute is a preoccupation with mere phenomena for which there is little scriptural warrant. How healthy the prospects are, if we discipline ourselves to stay within the guidelines laid down in the Word of God and learn to minister within them. By doing so I believe we could release the Church of God into a wonderful healing ministry. The Holy Spirit loves to use Christ's Body to this end. My experience is that many more will take it up providing they are not burdened by an expectation for total success which is more claimed than real. The ultimate responsibilities for the health and salvation are then left in safer hands than ours. God knows how to cope with all our insoluble problems. The community of faith continues in the midst, speaking of the One who never fails because He alone has conquered all, even death. His Name – Jesus. We also release a new factor in our evangelistic mission for Christ, for the healing of the sinner's sickness can often be the first stage to full salvation. This always includes the forgiveness of their sins and their deliverance from darkness. We shall look at this is the next chapter.

Healing

The Condition	Matt	Mark	Luke	John	Acts
A. ORGANIC DISORDERS					
Paralysis of Centurion's Servant	8.5		7.1		
Man with four friends	9.1	2.1	5.18		
Withered hand	12.10	3.1	6.6		
Woman with spondylitis			13.16		
Blind and lame	21.14				
Leprosy	8.2	1.40	5.12		
Ten lepers			17.12		
Fevers	8.14	1.30	4.38	4.47	
Blindness				9.1	
Bartimaeus	20.30	10.46	18.35		
Woman with issue	9.20	5.25	8.43		
Epilepsy	4.23 17.15				
The lame man at the gate					3.1
Paul's sight					9.9
Aeneas					9.22
Lystra					14.8
Fever/dysentry					28.3
B. DEMONIC					
Gadara	8.28	5.1	8.26		
Daughter of Syro-Phoenician	15.22	7.24			
Child	17.14	9.14	9.38		
Man with unclean spirit		1.23	4.33		
Mary Magdalene			8.22		

The Condition	Matt	Mark	Luke	John	Acts
Dumb	9.32				
Blind and dumb	12.22		11.14		
Multitudes		1.32,39			
		3.10			
	9.32	6.13			
Philippi					16.16
Sick and unclean spirits					5.16

C. NEUROTIC/ PSYCHOLOGICAL

Lunacy	4.24				
Anxiety	6.28				
	11.28				

D. RESUSCITATION

Jairus' daughter	9.18	5.22	8.41		
Widow of Nain			7.11		
Lazarus				11.1	
Tabitha					9.36–42
Eutychus					20.7–12

E. UNSPECIFIED AND GENERAL HEALINGS

A few sick	13.58	6.5			
Crowds	14.34				
	4.23–24				
	9.35		6.17		5.12–16
	14.14	6.55	9.11	6.2	8.5–8
Great crowds	15.30				19.11–12
	19.2				28.9

5

Discernment and the Ministry of Deliverance

Nowhere does the Bible encourage speculation into the activities of demons. In marked contrast to the modern assumption that unseen powers may be investigated without risk, we are warned frequently of their wicked plans. They have vast though finite intelligence like their leader whom Jesus describes as 'the prince of this world' (John 12.31). Following the example of the devil they specialise in an assortment of brazen lies that will confuse, or subtle lies that have just enough truth in them to be really dangerous. They use violence that will terrorise, temptations that will induce guilt if yielded to, and many other forms of destructive attack.

Christ's mission is set against the background of a titanic struggle with the devil and all his associates leading to a glorious victory through the cross and the resurrection. Since we live on this side of Calvary we share His triumph though through the reality of our present warfare. Until the day dawns on which Christ completes His triumph through His return, this world remains under the devil's influence (1 John 5.19). Since he knows how desperate the situation is for him he frequently manoeuvres to change the point of his attack. We are bound to fight him because we are certain to encounter him. Our success is assured providing we are adequately armed and alert (Ephesians 6.10–18).

We need feel no sympathy for the powers in revolt. But we do need to remember that in this form of warfare as in any other, truth is always the first casualty. The enemy launches a major offensive because he hates truth in all its forms. Sometimes truth is assaulted by those who should be its allies. It is here that the gift of discernment becomes even more significant. For we are guilty of this form of mutiny whenever we permit distortion, exaggeration or misleading information to lead us away from known or revealed facts. Many a Christian leader has lost his effectiveness in this way. Not only is discernment a means of sifting through our own self-deceptions it is also a God given facility for seeing how the devil has sprung the trap on us. This leads to deep repentance and forgiveness but also to determination not to be caught again another time. The worst reason for investigating this subject is a fascination for it. Better qualifications are a sound character, a good understanding of Scripture, mature discipleship and a well-tuned sense of humour. You need the latter not to deal with demons but to puncture the extravagant claims of the super-spiritual who spot demons everywhere.

Our rediscovery of the Christian deliverance ministry in the present day owes much to the discernment of a little known Lutheran pastor of the last century in Germany. His name was Johann Christoph Blumhardt and he ministered in Mottlingen from 1838–1852. It was whilst he was there that he became involved in helping a truly hopeless young woman in his charge, Gottlieben Dittus. She was dangerously demonised. It was only after an exhausting struggle lasting two years that she was set free from all that bound her to be restored to a sane normal and above all believing life. Her final release came with a phrase that expelled the last of the demons. It also expressed the confident message that Blumhardt subsequently preached with great effectiveness leading to many conversions, 'Jesus is Victor, Jesus is Victor.' So we approach the ministry of deliverance armed by the same assurance. There is not a devil or a demon around anywhere by whom Jesus can be overcome. On the contrary He and His Church share the same mandate to destroy the devil and all his works (1 John 3.8). We begin to do this by observing the signs which may betray the devil's influence.

The Evidence For Demons

The first sign of their presence is often that of a morbid absorption with the occult. This is a very broad term covering morally neutral activities such as water divining. It also speaks of 'the hidden things of life'. The general decline in institutional Christianity links with a phenomenal upsurge of interest in these areas. The daily horoscope is one example, now a standard feature in most magazines and in the popular press. Meditationalism is another. Yoga and Transcendentalism aim at the cultivation of a mind in a vacuum state which demons delight in. The Ouija has become a family game for many, though it is an activity which invokes the presence of the spirits. By far the most popular expression remains Spiritism. This practice encourages contact with what claim to be the spirits of the dead. In my experience no one who has been involved in Spiritism has enjoyed a satisfactory faith in Christ, without deliverance. Often their contact has been second-hand through parents or relatives but still they have needed some help. All these things are uncompromisingly rejected in Scripture. Those who enter into this forbidden zone are opening themselves up to the power of demons.

Obsessional behaviour patterns in any form are equally revealing. No one in their right senses will tend towards the depraved, the violent, the lustful or the mad. But to open oneself up to any of these can be spiritually disastrous, since demonic powers always exploit our human weaknesses. It is probable that it was by this means that the evil spirit oppressed the man in the Capernaum synagogue (Mark 1.23). Similarly, the man of Geresa with the legion was overwhelmed by violent spirits (Mark 5.2). I think of a Christian missionary who could not get out of his mind the scenes of an evil film full of vice and degradation. There was another who opened herself up to the demonic through cultivating rather than rejecting a root of bitterness in the soil of the soul (Hebrews 12.15). But the unclean spirits of pornography and anger must yield to Jesus. This was the case with Gordon who had turned to homosexuality when he found that his wife was unfaithful to him. He came into Christ's freedom when an angry demon was expelled in the Name of Jesus. It was not an unclean spirit as might have been suspected. But obsessions are many and varied. All of them yield to the power of Christ who is stronger than the strong.

Severe mental depressions may indicate bondage. In its most acute form, depression can be suicidal. If the sufferer has undergone great stress in their childhood their condition is no great surprise. They will need much inner healing. But we should be on the look-out for signs of the blighting influence of evil powers. If they are present then inner healing on its own will never bring the release that is sought. The case of King Saul is an example of one who was chronically depressed. His condition worsened through demonic influence (1 Samuel 15.22; 16.14). With his will weakened by this means he sought guidance from the witch of Endor. Later he died, virtually a suicide through misery combined with persecution mania and his disobedience (1 Chronicles 10.13). Demons enjoy exploiting this condition to the full.

Many Christians are among those who are in the grip of sinful habits which deny the Lord to whom they belong. Though the practices may be comparatively trivial it is their inevitability which makes them so distressing and a sign of satanic influence. For instance, I have always sought to lift a heavy burden of guilt from young people who have sought help in escaping from the practice of masturbation. In the teenage years it is often little more than a natural stage in the process of their own self discovery. It is also true that evangelical preachers have unfairly used this stage of development as a good means to bring about conviction of sin, but although most grow out of it in the course of their development it can lead to a condition in which the sufferer can almost hear the mocking laughter of demons. Their victims need the firm help of the Lord in breaking the hold of these unclean spirits. They can then hold their heads high again. Christ's victory applies just as much to habits of word and thought as here. But this is a common bondage.

An ambivalence towards Jesus and God often indicates demonic oppression. The girl in Philippi with a spirit of prediction is a good example of this (Acts 16.16). Perhaps this spirit had come upon her through the pagan influences of worship at the Delphic shrines. It is literally 'a spirit, a python'. This is the name of the mythical dragon who was the guardian to the Oracles and was reputed to have been slain by Apollo in the Greek legends. In due course it becomes a title for the spirit which inspires prediction. The girl is both attracted and repelled by the Apostles until the spirit is rebuked and expelled at Paul's command. We can see the same process at work with the Gerasene. In their case, the demons show a fearful awareness of the inevitability of their fate. They are always firm believers in God. 'Have you come here to torture us before the appointed time?' they ask (Matthew 8.29). Yet the man himself comes close to Jesus as if fascinated by him (Mark 5.6). It is by no means evident that those with evil spirits will want to distance themselves from Church, Christians or Christ. On the contrary we may expect that they will draw near without ever being able to complete the journey in a spiritual sense. First they must receive Christ's word of release and then they will be able to come to Him.

Physical sickness can be caused by demonic attack. The Gospel writers are careful to show that not all sickness is directly related to such assaults any more than it is to specific acts of sin. That makes the other references all the more significant. One man is dumb because of a demon (Matthew 9.32). Another blind for the same reason (Matthew 12.22). Epilepsy is associated with the demonic elsewhere (Luke 9.42). A woman with a spinal complaint is described as 'one whom satan has bound' (Luke 13.16). In each of these instances physical healing accompanies their deliverance. We can readily understand this when the cause of the disease is diagnosed as being of the psychosomatic kind. Allergies, ulcers, and heart troubles can be included in that category. The complaint and the cure are no less real for those reasons. The healing is wonderful when it is without any other treatment than that of the Name of the Lord.

Why Bondage Occurs

Symptoms of this condition are many and varied as we can see. We need to bear in mind that we know little or nothing about the origin of demonic spirits. Scripture is all but silent on this theme. When it comes to the means by which they gain access there are clearer indications. As we have seen, a primary reason is through allowing Satan a foothold by dabbling in the realms in which his rule still operates. Paul warns of the danger of this (Ephesians 4.27). Unresolved anger can soon give the devil a foothold which will become a springboard. This is plainly the case with Nebuchadnezzar who suffers a form of madness because of his sinful rebellion (Daniel 4.27). To trifle with sin in any form is to become exposed to fearful possibilities. In addition to this general danger we should take due note of some more specific threats that come to us through confusing the psychic with the spiritual. Paul reveals to us that the man of sin who is yet to appear will be an expert at producing 'counterfeit miracles, signs and wonders' (2 Thessalonians 2.9). By the term psychic we refer to phenomena outside the domain of natural law which are not the result of God's activity but which are stirred up from within our baser selves. Adolph Hitler is an example of one whose psyche became the means by which the devil's purposes were fulfilled. According to Alan Bullock there is not much evidence for Hitler's supposed commitment to astrology. Others take a different view and this was undoubtedly the case for his propaganda minister Goebbels. At the same time Bullock goes to some lengths to understand Hitler's strange and mesmeric quality over his audience by means of a capacity for instinctive sensitivity. He quotes Otto Strasser, one of Hitler's bitterest critics thus: 'Hitler responds to the vibration of the human heart with the delicacy of the seismograph or perhaps a wireless receiving set enabling him with a certainty with which no conscious gift could endow him to act as a loud-speaker proclaiming the most secret desires, the least admissible instincts, the sufferings and personal revolts of the whole nation.' 'It is', says Bullock 'like the occult acts of the African medicine man or the Asiatic Shaman . . . a medium or a hypnotist.' When we consider the horrors of the Second World War it is not hard to conclude that Europe underwent a fearful process of demonisation at this time through Hitler. The irony is that he liked to think of himself as a faith healer. He had made his inner soul freely available and the devil did the rest.

There are these demon forces which have controlled our modern history according to Oscar Cullman and Paul Tillich. Many modern theologians are taking a renewed interest in their evil effectiveness. Nazism, McCarthyism and Apartheid point up the relevance of such a study according to C.E.B. Cranfield. Whilst I am concentrating on discernment and the demonic in the pastoral dimension, the major task of the Church has to do with exposing and exorcising these major powers in today's society. We must not neglect the evidence of their activity in the minor fail-ures of our Christian living. The absence of adequate personal vigilance exposes us to great danger insists the Apostle Paul. We need to put on God's complete armour (Ephesians 6.10–18). It is a way of saying that we can be totally protected from head to foot through the merits of Christ and His salvation, but if we do not arm ourselves with Christ's goodness we are vulnerable.

Our responsibilities for this are not confined only to ourselves. The New Testament emphasises the corporate nature of Christian protection because it knows nothing of a faith which is without a concern for the welfare of others in the Body of Christ. So we are to encourage one another.

We are also to give each other admonishment (Hebrews 10.25; 1 Thessalonians 5.12; Colossians 3.16). This means a loving concern for each other through which we strengthen our resolve to serve the Lord and expose the compromises through which we fail Him. The need for this is heightened by the days in which we live. Bad as they are, Paul's view is that they are likely to get worse before God's Day finally comes (1 Timothy 4.1; 2 Timothy 3.1). It is all due to the power of 'deceiving spirits and demons'. So we need to guard each other's flanks at the time as we are all members of Christ. The purpose is for release not condemnation. Churches need to develop relationships of mutual accountability and openness if such a process is easily fulfilled.

We are liable to demonic attack because the outside world conpires together with the inner cravings of our own flesh. Outside of Christ it is a fact that organised life on planet earth is naturally ungodly. It is under the power of the enemy. We ourselves are similarly attracted to the base and sinful because of our fallen human nature. This does not mean that the devil attacks only through sensuality – 'the cravings of a sinful man, the lust of his eyes and the boast of what he has or does' (1 John 2.16). He also uses loneliness, apathy, despondency, avarice, doubt, weakness, failure and fear of his purposes. There are many who are held by such enemies which exercise their power through pathos or pride. Apathy and fear seem particularly strong in inner city areas like Inner London, paralysing many new initiatives for God. Sometimes failure is a family heritage. It is a curse that is upon a family to the third and fourth generation of the guilty. It can only be lifted through the application of Christ's healing grace who loves to forgive wickedness, rebellion and sin when we repent of it. Grace always remains stronger than sin. 'Sin shall not be your master because you are not under law, but under grace' (Romans 6.14). Because the devil and his servants assume the role of being accusers they never like to be reminded of the basic Gospel terms which assure us of freedom as well as forgiveness in Christ.

Treatment With Care

In order to bring others into the release of Christ we must make it clear that the victims have our full support and love. We are neither angry with them nor are we wanting to attack them personally. Words of reassurance about this are always needed because demons foster misery and false guilt. This is all the more necessary if we are likely to become firmly authoritative in our dealings with the powers. Jesus always establishes a rapport with their victims but none with the demons. We must follow His example. We will soon perceive that people are demonised to different degrees. John Richards uses the terms demonic influence, oppression, attack and mediumship or possession in an ascending scale of seriousness for them. In the Scriptures the more general term which covers all is to say that they are demonised. However critical the presence of the spirit is, it is always necessary to secure the active co-operation of the one concerned if they are to know lasting release.

In my experience there are five steps in their deliverance.

a) *Take authority.* In this ministry it is not a case of humble dependence as in the prayer 'Lord please set him free from all that troubles him.' For the Lord has told us to release the prisoner in His Name. Hence with confident faith we say 'In Jesus Name I release you from all that troubles you now.' Demons are swift to spot a failure in faith at this point and we need to make sure that we are moving with the confidence that God gives.

b) *Identify the need.* Scripture indicates differing characteristics among evil spirits. They all share a common capacity to deceive. They are all intelligent, unclean, vicious, and have the power to contaminate. They take up all the weaknesses to which we have referred earlier from apathy through to fear and can, on occasions, display amazing strength. Quite recently I experienced this again when a mere slip of a girl was brought into a church vestry for prayer after a service. She lunged at me with astonishing speed and made an attempt at strangling me. Obviously it was not successful and she was brought to an abrupt halt when I called on the Name of the Lord Jesus. He stopped her in her tracks and also restored my shattered cool. As the prayer time proceeded I think she left the vestry with less in her than was there when she came. But this sort of ministry can often be surprising and nerve-wracking. When you hear a demon's sneering laugh it can make you feel quite weak. We should be on the watch for a spirit of guilt masquerading as true Christian sorrow. It is nothing of the kind, for it only produces a worldly grief leading to death. Outwardly pious it may be. But inwardly this sorrow is a device for a religious spirit as proud as Lucifer but as miserable as hell.

c) *Bind them*. That means restrict their activity by the power of Christ's cross, resurrection and ascension. The sad caricature in the modern horror story is that of a pathetic priest, usually morally compromised and vainly waving his crucifix before a ghastly all-powerful phantom. Jesus says that we may tie up the strong man before we spoil his house (Matthew 12.29). We also have a responsibility for what we prohibit or permit (Matthew 16.19; 18.18). This Rabbinic phrase refers to the capacity of the Church to forgive people their sins or refuse forgiveness because of their lack of repentance. It also carries with it the right to affirm Christ's access and bar that of Satan's to people for whom we pray.

d) *Expel them*. Demons recognise Christ and acknowledge His right to rule them. This is clear in Christ's encounters as they are described in the Gospels. 'Have you come to destroy us? I know whom you are, the Holy one of God' (Mark 1.24). 'Swear to God that you won't touch me' (Mark 5.7). 'You deaf and dumb spirit come out of him and never enter him again . . . the spirit shrieked and came out' (Mark 9.25–26). It is never a matter of argument or debate. It is not even a case of making sure about getting the verbal formula correct. This is a pressing concern for professional exorcists but not for Jesus. The verb used is *ekballein* and literally it means 'to chuck out.' That is what Jesus and the apostles did often unceremoniously.

e) *Seal up the gaps*. Having evicted the demons like unwanted tenants it is important that the house is not left unoccupied. Jesus warns of this danger. There are spiritual squatters around and a house swept clean and in good order will become a haven for other spirits more wicked than the original one. The last state will then be worse than the first (Matthew 12.45). The most trusted tenant for our innermost being is Christ's Other Self, the Holy Spirit. When He comes in He introduces love, joy, peace and all the other spiritual characteristics that will beautify His dwelling place. We can never have too much of Him. Yet He is so courteous, gracious and self effacing. For He focuses all the attention not on himself but on Christ.

We had a desperate experience once with a demonised man who refused the presence of the Holy Spirit once he had been released. It seemed incredible but his reason was theological. Though he was in the grip of sin and vice he held to a view about the Spirit of God which he had learned in his youth, that the Spirit and His gifts were confined to the first dispensation and were not for now. Alex came to me late on a Saturday night and he was roaring drunk. To tell the truth I too was a little heady since my sermons for the next day were still in a state of disarray and time was marching on. My first job was to attempt to silence his piteous cries for help. When at last this was achieved I took the authority of Christ and ordered alcoholism out of him. Without much struggle it left him and I was able to take home a remarkably sober man even though his breath still smelt abominably. He came back on several occasions after this. God gave me an insight into the cause of his troubles. It had come about through his cohabiting with a prostitute who was also a spiritualist. He sought forgiveness for all this but would not on any account go further in terms of receiving the Holy Spirit. A few months later he did come back but a broken man. He had been driving his lorry on the main A74 trunk road from Glasgow south and had given a lift to two hitch hikers. When they saw him guzzling neat vodka they soon wanted another vehicle. They informed the police and Alex was picked up further down the road. Put into the police cells to dry out he took off his belt and made a noose with which to end it all, but was caught just in time. The poor sad broken man taught us this lesson. Never leave those who are delivered from an evil spirit unless they are filled with the Holy Spirit. To be filled with the Spirit is a must in deliverance ministry.

We should not ignore the *power of symbolism* and sacrament in deliverance. When our children were young we found this quite helpful on the occasions when their sleep was disturbed by troublesome dreams. We would comfort the little ones with a prayer, open a window and order the nasty dream out into the darkness of the night. The bang with which the window was then shut was quite sufficient to assure the child that they would not be troubled further and a peaceful night for all the household then followed. It is often the same when comforting and encouraging those who have been set free from worse entities than a bad dream. Quite apart from anything else they need healing. There never can be a better way than to share Christ with them afresh through the bread and the wine of the eucharist. It takes on a whole new meaning for those who have just renounced the world, the flesh and the devil. As they feed on Christ He occupies them fully and His presence is confirmed by this means of grace.

Discerning Deliverance

I believe in the need for corporate discernment in this ministry. We should never begin to engage in it on our own. We will need prayer support from others and it all takes a great deal of time. We need to be very practical about it. Never attempt it if you are overtired. Jesus snatches some sleep in the boat on Galilee in spite of a tempest and to the great consternation of His disciples (Mark 4.37). Not only was He already tired but He knew that He would need to be alert for the conflict of the next day in Geresa. So we should avoid the impression that demons are particularly vulnerable at 2.00 am. Actually it is the other way round, in that it is Christians who need their sleep at 2.00 am whereas demons are not particularly bothered. When we work as a team we find that the different members are sensitive to the different stages. You can check each other out in this way. You can keep each other on their toes, not attributing to demons what could be alternatively explained by natural factors.

The signs of the exit of demons are clear. Very often a physical sensation is experienced as this point is reached. They may feel a tightness in the chest or throat, or pain in the pit of the stomach. I recall one young man who felt himself being strangled. This was in our lounge at home. His yell at the exit of the demon caused our poor unsuspecting cocker spaniel to take off on all four legs simultaneously, but she was soon restored to her customary sleepy calm. It had been an unnerving experience for her. Another young woman went through the motions of childbirth as she was released. She had been suffering from the side effects of spiritism in the family. Why they affected her in this particular way I do not know. It is at times like this that people may collapse in a heap on the floor. There may be a lot of noise although it is my view that it should be restricted, certainly in a public meeting. It was in the Capernaum synagogue that Jesus told the evil spirit to be muzzled when it was shouting out (Mark 1.25)! It is not healthy to encourage a cacophony as good supporting evidence of the validity of the ministry. It only encourages the unstable to carry on alarmingly because they have been given licence to do so.

The real evidence of release is in four qualities which begin to shine through.

a) *Peace*. With God, with others and also with themselves. God's *shalom* descends upon the free.

b) *Beauty*. They were never more ugly than when they were tormented. They are never more beautiful than when they have come through. It is an inner serenity which owes nothing to cosmetics and everything to grace.

c) *Right mindedness.* It was so for the man in Geresa (Mark 5.15). Now they are free to exercise their true humanity, to be and to think as a child of God.

d) *Openness to God.* Since they are free they now want to walk with Him as their best companion and chief joy. The prayer life of the released is an inspiration for God does most of the talking. They listen and act in the light of what they hear, and so answer many of their own petitions.

Using our discernment in this ministry we can see that it is always important that those who are released are sustained. They will need warm fellowship from a supportive church which has a real understanding for them. No one would think of attaching a live chick to a dead hen and the key to wholeness is a caring ministry through which more healing may continue. Caring churches need the meat of God's living Word if they are to grow strong enough to begin an attack on the evil powers of an evil age. For we have only considered our warfare over a limited front. Feeding on the Word is a crucial issue in the growth of perception. We will look at this next.

6

Discernment and Scripture

Good scriptural ministries produce sound discerning churches. The teaching of the Word of God remains a priority for which there is no substitute. It cannot be skimped without the most lamentable consequences. It is a demanding exercise both in the giving and the receiving of it. For the Bible is a work of the Spirit for spiritual ends. When it is expounded to us we are exposed to a force which is remarkably informing, transforming, convicting and inspiring. So it has been for the Church throughout the centuries. 'There is nothing useless or superfluous in the writings even if they seem obscure', says Origen. Augustine said that 'the Holy Scripture can neither be deceived nor deceive.' Calvin could have been speaking for all the great reformers when he declared 'No man can have the least knowledge of true and sound doctrine without having been a disciple of Scripture.' 'The Holy Scriptures are able to make you wise for salvation through faith in Christ Jesus', says Paul (2 Timothy 3.15). In short, Christians never mature spiritually without the aid of the Bible.

Put the other way round it is also true. *The gift of discernment feeds upon sound teaching*. It is the Word of God which gives the objective standards by which we can measure the difference between right and wrong, good and bad, the good and the best, God's will and our own ideas. This is the point according to the writer of the Hebrews 'The solid food (of God's Word) is for the mature, who by constant use have trained themselves to distinguish good from evil' (Hebrews 5.14). Scripture provides us with many examples of the gift of discernment in action. Of course, God could have delivered a very different Bible to us in a series of theological propositions. He did not choose to do so. Instead, He used the experiences of many different people. By this means the Bible encourages us to learn from their example and thus grow in the gift. Writing to the Romans Paul says 'Everything that was written in the past was written to teach us, so that through endurance and the encouragement of the Scriptures we might have hope' (Romans 15.4). The Scriptures accurately describe many of the living situations of the Church today where discernment is needed. The letters to the seven churches in Revelation 2 and 3 are an example. Each church is different. They are as varied in their social setting, in their virtues, sins and opportunities as churches are today. Yet Christ reads them all as we would say – like a book. Each letter exposes a real situation and conveys God's living Word into it. We can never manage without Scripture. Without Scripture there is no discernment. Whatever wisdom we may have known, we swiftly lose if it is not sustained by Bible truth.

In order to grasp this relationship between discerment and Scripture further, we need to consider some first principles about the Bible. Do we really need one, and if so, why?

The Purposes of the Bible

The Bible's answer to this question is that it was written *in order to build faith amongst those who read it*. Scripture does this in many different ways but I will refer to only two. Firstly, it is full of the most thrilling testimonies to God's faithfulness to His own people. In the Old Testament we are given numerous examples of this. Our faith is to rest on God's faithfulness. The story of Abraham tells us how God honours all His promises to the patriarch. The Exodus story describes how He delivers His own faithless people from what appears to be inevitable slavery in Egypt. God keeps His Covenant with Moses and Israel for no other reason than that He cannot break it. For He is the God of the Covenant. It is no different in the New Testament. God's faithfulness is demonstrated through God's Son. Every instance in His Life declares this, including even crucifixion, followed by resurrection and ascension. Every doctrine conveys the same message of the faithfulness of God. So Christian faith is not a quality drawn out of us by an act of our own will. It is never any use to urge people to this or upbraid them because they don't respond. To do that is to show that we have never properly understood what faith is all about in the first instance. Faith is a quality which draws all its strength from the one in whom it is placed. A slender timber on its own never has strength. It can be quite adequate however, if it rests securely on two strong adjacent rocks which bear its load. The testimony of the two Testaments to the faithfulness of God will do marvels for the weakest plank of faith providing we rely on the character of God to which they bear witness.

Secondly, the Bible builds faith through its intriguing witness to the potential faith releases. Once we start to trust in a God who is faithful, the Bible tells us that anything God wants for us can actually happen. That is what Christ means by the repeated promises 'Anything you ask . . . in My Name' (John 14.14; 15.16; 16.23). Not in fact that this is an invitation for us to ask for all the selfish expedients that easily arise uppermost in our minds. The phrase 'in My Name' forbids that. The blank cheque must still bear Christ's signature if heaven is to honour it. Ours won't do. But if it is all in accordance with God's purpose however, there is nothing that will be denied us. Our faith will grow, stimulated by the many encouragements of Scripture. We will be changed by this means from the self-centred beings we are by nature into the Christ-centred believers we may become by grace. The Scriptures will have done their job because their focus is always Christ. We would never have known Him at all without the Word of God.

The Bible is also vital because it is *the means for imparting knowledge to us*. Whilst there is often a supernatural element about discernment, as we have already seen there is also an intellectual base which must not be overlooked. God's self revelation both in Christ and through the Scriptures, and through His mighty acts is never wordless. To take but one example. One of the most amazing deliverances for Israel was during the reign of King Hezekiah. Sennacherib King of Assyria was poised to overthrow Hezekiah's defences, storm and sack the city of Jerusalem and pull it down. Hezekiah was in the besieged city and sought the aid of the Prophet Isaiah. Quite suddenly God intervened. We are told in 2 Kings 19.35 'That night the angel of the Lord went out and put to death a hundred and eighty five thousand men in the Assyrian camp. When the people got up the next morning – there were all the dead bodies.' From then on there could never be any ambiguity as far as Israel was concerned. The action was clear, and so too the explanation of what God had done.

God gave this word to us because like Hezekiah we are all rational beings. It is part of what it means to be made in the image of God. Paul tells us that the gathering of information is important for our discernment. 'And this is my prayer', he writes to the Philippians, 'that your love may abound more and more in knowledge and depth of insight, so that you may be able to discern what is best, and may be pure and blameless on the day of Christ' (Philippians 1.9–10). Again to the Colossians: 'We have not stopped praying for you and asking God to fill you with knowledge of His Will through all spiritual wisdom and understanding' (Colossians 1.9). The consequences are, that we will be 'renewed in knowledge in the image of the Creator' (Colossians 3.10). We will have put on the new self. Since the Bible is the source book for all this, Paul is simply indicating again the need to read it. It is not spiritual day dreaming which he is commending, nor is it to divide off the activities of the mind from the supposedly higher activities of the spirit as some would teach. That is a basic misunderstanding about soul and spirit which leads to many practical problems in due course. It is solid, wise, joyful, discriminating and even theological study. Many misleading doctrines which begin with the rejection of thought lead in the end to claims for the special revelations of their teachers which straightforward Bible teaching would never allow. The more we know the Word of God the less trouble we will have with the Will of God. Paul writes to Timothy in his first letter with a relevant admonition to devote himself to the public reading of Scripture (1 Timothy 4.13). Astonishing as it may seem, there are many churches today which make much of their scriptural orthodoxy but who scarcely read Scripture publicly at all. Or if they do so, almost invariably they read it appallingly badly. But in his second letter Paul returns to this theme with even greater significance. 'From infancy you have known the Holy Scriptures which are able to make you wise to Salvation through Christ Jesus. All Scripture is God breathed and is useful for teaching, rebuking, correcting, training in righteousness, so that the man of God may be thoroughly equipped for every good work' (2 Timothy 3.15–16). The Scriptures build up the resources of our understanding on which wise judgments can be safely based.

It is through the teaching of the Bible that we can overcome the *poisonous suggestions of the devil*. In times of increased activity by the Spirit of God, we have already seen that the enemy is even more determined to lead God's people astray. We have noticed many of his schemes with a carefully placed half truth. Effectively it becomes a great lie. He is also adept at the selective use of Scripture and we will need to look at its proper use a little further on. Suffice to say, that Jesus does not deal with the tendency by ignoring Scripture. Rather the reverse. From proof texts, He goes to major principles through which all Scripture should be interpreted (Matthew 4.4; 7.10). Whatever stategy the devil may adopt, it is the contents of the Bible that supply the answer that will overcome him. If fear is his weapon, faith is the answer. 'God has not given us the spirit

of fear, but power, love and self control.' To guilt and
unworthiness the Word responds 'There is therefore now
no condemnation for those who are in Christ Jesus'
(Romans 8.1). To the most distressing pressure for modern
people, anxiety. 'Do not worry about your life, your body,
food, drink, clothing . . . and tomorrow', says Jesus, ' . . .
Your Heavenly Father knows you need these things'
(Matthew 6.25ff).

The Scriptures also give us the *message of the Gospel to
communicate to those who do not yet know Christ*. We are
not likely to establish a link with our contact by spotting a
secret message written upon their anatomy with invisible
ink. God does give unusual insights from time to time. Paul
says that our appeal is to their conscience through plainly
setting forth the truth of Christ (2 Corinthians 4.2). It is all
without self commendation (2 Corinthians 5.12). Since we
are attempting to 'persuade men' (v.11) out of the fear of
the Lord – we are applying the message of the Scripture to
their condition. This was Paul's normal evangelistic method
and it was mightily effective. He writes thus to the Thessalonians: 'We thank God continually because when you
received the Word of God which you heard from us, you
accepted it, not as the word of men, but as it actually is,
the Word of God which is at work in you who believe' (1
Thessalonians 2.13). Not surprisingly it is still those who
have a high view of the inspiration and reliability of Scripture who are effective in evangelism. Their message gains
decisive authority because its basis is clear.

With all this, the purpose of the Scripture in short is to
bring us to a right mind and so to mature judgment. The
Scriptures insist on the need for intellectual activity. They
also provide us with the raw material for our thoughts which
will lead us to perceptive conclusions. Our mind will be
renewed. We will be like the spiritual man described by the
Apostle as one who 'makes judgments about all things,
though he himself is not subject to any judgment . . . with
the mind of Christ' (1 Corinthians 2.15–16). As mature
people we will take a view on things as Paul puts it. It

means that we will be characterised by our independence of thought. Our minds will be motivated by the best reasons, 'set on things above, not on earthly things' (Colossians 3.2). Scripture describes all these processes and it also provides a stimulant through which they may occur. It is not enough to speak of the value of the Scriptures for this, for they are indispensable. The more we work at the job of rightly handling the Scriptures, the greater our spiritual insight will become. The Scriptures are not of course, a compendium of all information. They are the source that really matters as far as the things of faith are concerned. John Wesley's testimony to this needs to be heard again. 'I want to know one thing, the way to heaven; how to land safe on that happy shore. God Himself has condescended to teach that way . . . He has written it down in a book – O give me that book! At any price give me the book of God!'

Building Discernment through Scripture

Since the Scripture is designed for these purposes we need to consider some further practical implications. The reading of Scripture releases immensely constructive potential for us providing we do it in the right way. The first guideline is to *allow Scripture to speak as its authors intended it to*. We need to know something about the background to the passage. Is the author a poet or an historian? If he is a prophet, to whom is his message directed? To what extent is he correcting an abuse, or stating an unchanging principle? It has frequently been claimed that you can prove anything from the Bible. With such a variety of writing, styles, authors and historical backgrounds and purposes that is probably true. Hermeneutics – the right interpretation of Scripture in the light of its many background factors – is essential for our scriptural claims to be valid. In making this point about the serious study of any passage I must add the need for dealing with one passage at a time. Preachers who festoon their sermons with endless references to other texts fail at this point. Each Scripture has its own weight and must be allowed to contribute to our understanding accordingly. Some Bible reading notes are of questionable merit for this reason. If they always return to the one theme that the writer is always making, you will do better without them, armed with your own notebook and pencil.

The Bible will build up our capacity to judge wisely when *we balance Scripture with Scripture*. There are passages in the Old Testament that are scarcely appropriate for regular public reading. I still recall the looks of surprise, turning to horror and then glee when one of my Assistants launched into just such a section of the Law in the Old Testament one Sunday morning. It deals with improper sexual relationships within the family and is very explicit. Needless to say this was the wrong chapter. The Bible has much beautiful teaching on the important subject of sexuality besides prohibitions about stripping . . . ! The reason why we jettison the Old Testament teaching on the death penalty for a variety of offences is not because we have become morally soft. Nor is it because we despise the important principle of judgment which is being made here. It is because of the Biblical stress on the fallibility of our judgment but the righteousness of God's. 'It is mine to avenge, I will repay says the Lord' (Romans 12.19). The practice of Levirate marriages falls on the same principle. It is referred to in Deuteronomy 25.5–10 as a means of making provision for the childless widow. She may yet become a mother through her brother-in-law. Any child is taken to be in the name of the dead brother 'So that his name will not be blotted out from Israel.' The practice is seen to be invalid in the light of the much broader and weightier teaching about the exclusive lifelong union between one man and one wife. So we make our judgments in the light of this.

To follow this up I add that we should teach Scripture in the light of both its principles and its trends before we pursue the teaching of stray texts. It is not the diversity of the message of Scripture which is uppermost but its harmony. Given that on every significant subject to do with faith and practice the Bible has got important things to say, we first need to understand the whole pattern. Then we need to see where they are leading. Then we weigh the contribution of diverging passages. It was by this means that the early Fathers developed their theology about the Trinity. It is by this means that we reject flimsy teaching such as the doctrine now out of vogue that you baptise only in the Name of Jesus. In other words, for discernment we need good biblically based theology. The downgrading of such serious study is never wise. In almost every case it is a public admission of the need for much more of it on the part of whoever is making cheap jibes in this respect.

We grow in discernment as *we allow for the dynamism of Scripture*. The Bible is not a static book. The word Paul uses about Scripture demands attention from the Timothy passage already quoted. It is *Theopneustos*. Literally it means 'God breathed' (2 Timothy 3.16). 'Inspired' will not do for that really means what is breathed in, whereas what Paul is insisting is the opposite. Scripture is what God breathed out. That means that having conceived Scripture, He initiates Scripture and communicates it. He speaks through Scripture. 2 Peter 1.21 helps us further. Concerning Scripture prophecy we are told that 'men spoke from God as they were carried along by the Spirit.' The Holy Spirit who carried those prophets now bears their readers. Thus the question which emerges from the reading of Scripture in the light of all its contents is, what is the Spirit saying to us now through this passage? Its timeless message faithfully expounded within its own context begins to seize hold of our consciences. The Spirit betrays his presence by always glorifying Christ. As He takes hold of His own familiar words Jesus comes alive to us once more, calling us, examining us, encouraging us or challenging us. The Word of God like a two edged sword has done its penetrating work. He sees this and so too do we. We never see things right unless this happens. We need to read Scripture regularly, thoughtfully, prayerfully and reflectively. It is never dull. I return to the value of reading it with a notebook and pencil poised. The most familiar passages light up in a fresh way as we open our hearts and minds to its teaching.

Using Scripture in Discernment

We have already referred to two dangerous characteristics in many churches through introspection and pragmatism. When it comes to the means by which we gather information for the direction of our lives, there are several other practices which need to be examined in the light of the Scripture and its teaching. Three examples will show how effectively the Scriptures do this.

Lively Christians, aflame with zeal, are often liable to a condition I call *illuminism*. By this I mean the inward conviction which takes control of them through their own spiritual insight, vision, revelation or perception. In the Scriptures we are left in no doubt that there is a high value to such experiences. Paul himself speaks of being caught up into heaven where he heard inexpressible things which he was not to reveal. Yet claims to such encounters need to be handled with great care, if they are the grounds upon which other claims stand. They are often just another way by which one Christian, often a leader, can seek far too much support for his own opinion. Illuminism allows us to close our mind to contributions coming from any other source and therefore justifies arrogance.

The balance of Scripture is that we test out the personal convictions to which we have come by the discernment of other Christians with whom we are already in fellowship. In this way instead of cultivating closed convictions, we will seek corporate discernment. The first Church Council in Jerusalem in Acts 15 is a good example of the robust ways in which we can arrive at consensus views. Admittedly it involved sharp debate, (v.2), much discussion, (v.7), silent attention, (v.12), careful reflection, (v.15), before they came to the conclusion 'It seemed good to the Holy Spirit and to us.' Tough though these processes can be they should not be ill-humoured or ugly. Corporate discernment breeds strong conviction and has solid merit for the whole Church family because it is honest, open and personally affirming. Having faced critical issues and come to a view on them it is infinitely stronger than views superimposed upon our consciences from others which have never really passed through the filter of our own mind and thinking. Although God has a personal plan for all of us, the Scriptures never allow us to believe that we are the only ones to hear Him speak. Illuminism is a spiritual malady to which all modern prophets are prone. They need the balancing help of a discerning people if they are to avoid the dangers of a terminal disease, and if their ministry is to be valuable to those who receive it.

Some churches are in danger of *fresh sectarianism*. From my own tradition I think I understand something of this approach and a little church history helps here. It is a valid church tradition to be in quest for the pure Church. We want to encourage the Church to her destiny as the beautiful Bride of Christ. Appropriate as this is, the new sectarians are often intent upon taking things a stage further than my own dissenting Baptist forebears would go. They also recognised Christ wherever He may be seen, and this bred a strong and surprising ecumenical spirit which their descendants have maintained to this day. This is the point that the new sectarians will have none of. Christ is with them and scarcely at all elsewhere. Often they come from those with the loosest denominational ties, so they call a plague down on those whose traditions are stronger. If they themselves have emerged from an independent stock which is isolationist there is nothing new about this for them. It's just that they have not given enough attention to the history of other churches or their trends. As someone has wisely remarked: 'Those who do not bother with history are condemned to relive it.' There are many sad instances in which a few go further still by enticing Christians away from churches which have nurtured them to join the new fellowships they have just founded which are, of course, always totally right – until they split yet again.

The spirit which Scripture encourages does not behave thus, since the Bible encourages relationships with all who belong to Christ. Love is to be the dominant quality amongst Christ's disciples, not scorn. Since the development of the Protestant missionary movement from the eighteenth century we have come to a greater respect for other Christian churches which is increasingly significant. Modern ecumenism is one expression of this. Charismatic renewal is another. We have begun to learn that whatever valuable insights God has given to us, we are bound to share with others. We are uniting together in mission for Christ out of an obedience to Scripture's imperatives. For we have come to understand that the vision for the *pure Church* needs to be set alongside the *prayer for the one Church*. We understand that Christ regards our divisions as a primary barrier to our evangelism. It is Scripture which shows up the inadequacy of fresh separatism since division is an ugly blemish on the face of Christ's Bride. The world will only believe when they see our oneness (John 17.21).

God's Word also reveals the weakness of *a new hedonism*. By this I refer to the teaching which stresses our happiness as the greatest goal of the Gospel. One of its forms is through the promise of great financial prosperity. Another of its forms is the promise of perfect health, and yet a third is that of freedom not only from sin's guilt but also from its potential here in this life. These teachings encourage a detachment from the pressing realities of the world which we are bound to face. They are given by preachers who start with the premise that spiritual knowledge from Scripture is different from the plain knowledge received by the kind of serious study I have been advocating. They are often supported by those whose circumstances stimulate a desire for better worldly things without too much clarity about the means by which they may be achieved.

Armed with the Scriptures it should not take us long to see through this. It is right to say that Christians are called to a life of faith in a faithful God. There is no question of our Father's commitment to supply all our needs out of His riches in glory in Christ Jesus (Philippians 4.19). Paul is confident that God underwrites every faith endeavour that He inspires, particularly when it is directed to the cause of His mission here. Yet we bear in mind that Paul was also aware of his own imminent death later on. In the same letter he says 'I am being poured out like a drink offering on the sacrifice and service coming from your faith. I am glad and rejoice with all of you.' He returns to the same phrase in 2 Timothy 4.6, and adds 'the time has come for my departure: I have fought the good fight. I have kept the faith. Now there is in store for me a crown of righteousness.' God's word to Paul is not prosperity but martyrdom. In all probability it was the same for Peter. To follow Christ meant the loss of all things as well as immense gain. The Bible teaches that tribulation, pain and suffering are still part of God's teaching methods as He prepares His people for glory. I do not believe that unthinking submission to the views of other Christians is ever the meaning of discipleship. The Bible teaches us to give ourselves over entirely to God. Perhaps the Church will only learn the costliness of this when the price of faith in the Western world is much higher than it is today, and we do battle with the powers.

The Scriptures rightly interpreted bring us to sound conclusions and clear perceptions. What happens if we attempt our discernment without them? The prophet Amos gives a vivid picture of what people are like where there is such a famine of hearing and receiving the words of the Lord. 'Men stagger from sea to sea and wander from North to East searching for the Word of the Lord, but they will not find it' (8.11). Hungry and directionless, a Church deprived of a sound understanding staggers from one opinionated prophecy to the next. Its members then topple into the grave of despondency from which very few ever rise. 'They will fall, never to rise again', says Amos. The immense danger of this false hedonism is not that of disappointment alone. It is rather that of the destruction of faith through preaching an unbalanced message that is bound to lead to disillusionment. Paul shows us a similar fate with 'infants tossed back and forth by the waves, blown here and there by every wind of teaching by the cunning and craftiness of men in their deceitful scheming.' We cannot follow the Lord at all without obedience to His Word, which we need properly explained and fully understood and acted on. On the issues on which it is silent, we make up our own minds in the light of our understanding of Christ. The history and experience of the people of God throughout the centuries is always a help. With our own convictions we submit to the final authority of Scripture, with our revelations we test all things by the Word of God. It is the Scriptures which bring us to sound judgments in the things of God.

7

Discernment and Revelations

God made man in His own image in order to enjoy human company. This is the Bible's teaching on our creation by a transcendent God who is holy and mysterious, yet also affectionate, intimate and personal. Our attitude to Him is to be marked by respect and confidence. Jesus uses the title 'Father' for God. He encourages us to do likewise. Through faith in Jesus we are admitted into the Father's family. We become brothers and sisters to each other. We share a common life and identity inspired by the Holy Spirit. We speak to God our Father in our prayers. He speaks to us in ways that we soon recognise as unique and unmistakable. At its heart there is always this two way communication in praying. This capacity to discern His voice is granted to all who belong to Christ. It is a characteristic of each individual Christian. As we shall go on to see, it is also a corporate quality to be sought by the whole family of God. He is always prepared to speak to His people who are willing to listen to Him.

There are many ways in which God communicates with us. In this chapter we are going to consider some of them and look also at the means by which we can filter out the phoney.

Having already pointed out the primary place of Scripture in revelation in the last chapter it is only necessary to mention that every spiritual experience must be submitted to the scrutiny of God's Word. A further important qualification is that all fresh revelations communicate information about God or His ways that we would not otherwise know. Words which really say nothing at all about Him may be personally interesting, but they are trivial. Ambiguous words capable of many different interpretations are equally valueless, and no amount of pious phraseology alters this. So we want to know what each special word is saying in order to assess it. If God is speaking He will repeat His Word many times and ways until we have grasped it. We will now consider the most important of them.

Prophecy

God's Call to His Church at Pentecost is the call to *prophesy*. This is the reason for Peter's inspired quotation from Joel 2.28–32. 'In the last days God says, I will pour out my Spirit on all people. Your sons and daughters will prophesy, your old men will dream dreams, your young men will see visions. Even on my servants both men and women I will pour out my Spirit in those days and they will prophesy' (Acts 2.17–18). There is a sense in which every utterance declared forth on God's behalf is prophetic. As has been frequently remarked, prophecy is primarily a forthtelling activity as well as one of foretelling. Here we are confining ourselves to its limited modern usage as a spontaneous and direct communication inspired by the Holy Spirit. By a prophetic word in this sense God is speaking to the heart of the matter with unmistakable clarity.

There is a considerable Bible basis for such a practice. The mighty men of God in the Old Testament are those who serve as God's messengers the prophets. Their words were often directed from God to the whole nation and to the other nations as well. Sometimes they were specific to the rulers of Israel. They burnt the conscience with the fire of God's righteousness and summoned God's people to responsive faith and repentance. Yet the New Testament also lays a heavy emphasis on this ministry. Jesus had the reputation of being a prophet (Mark 6.15; 8.28; 14.65). It is quite clear that He regarded Himself in this way and described His ministry in these terms.

'Only in his own home town among his own relations and in his own house is a prophet without honour', He says in Mark 6.4. It is because He is a prophet that He reckons on dying in Jerusalem. 'Surely no prophet can die outside' (Luke 13.33). From the coming of the Spirit at Pentecost and onwards, the early Church received this ministry in its midst. One of the first examples is that of Agabus and his companions (Acts 11.27). Through their ministry to the infant Church in Antioch a relief action is launched for the Judean Church which was shortly to be affected by dire famine. Later on prophets together with teachers identify Barnabas and Saul for special ministry responsibility (Acts 13.1–2). Philip the Evangelist had four unmarried daughters who were prophetesses (Acts 21.9). Whilst Paul is staying in their home in Caesarea Agabus visits again and accurately prophesies Paul's future imprisonment. Timothy was also called to his ministry when the Elders gave a prophetic message about this to him (1 Timothy 4.14).

Paul has much to say about prophecy both through his own personal testimony and through his understanding of its mighty purposes. He sets a high standard when he confides his insight into the way in which uncircumcised Gentiles and circumcised Jews are heirs together of the promises in Christ Jesus, as 'the mystery made known to me by revelation' (Ephesians 3.3). Far from being a little comforting word to give added security to a Christian facing personal difficulties, true prophecy defines the nature of the Church in new, broad, inclusive and universal terms in Christ. The genuine word has to do with massive themes. It results in a change of direction for Paul's own life which the other apostles found startling. To take another example from Paul's experience of this gift there is the extraordinary event he describes in 2 Corinthians 12.3. He was caught up into paradise and is not sure whether this was a physical or a spiritual experience in or apart from his body. What he does know, is that he heard of 'inexpressible things, things that man is not permitted to tell.' Perhaps they are to do with the prospects for God's people he describes elsewhere. 'No eye has seen, nor ear has heard, no mind has conceived what God has prepared for those who love him.' Such disclosures do not describe a little movement of personal ecstasy for Paul would never waste words over such minor matters as that. Yet the wonder of it all is in what follows. Paul goes on to write of the way he has to wrestle with the Lord over 'a thorn in my flesh.' He pleaded with God three times to take it away but God's word was clear. 'My grace is sufficient for you for my power is made perfect in weakness.' Prophecy is revelation from God and of God which can be shattering. It is also to man and about his condition. It speaks immediately to all our human needs.

In Paul's teaching in 1 Corinthians 14 there are four positive functions to consider.

a) *Prophecy strengthens the Church*. It builds the Church up in faith. The Greek word *Oikodomeo* is taken from the construction site. It describes house building. Earlier on in the same letter he has spoken about the poor quality materials that may be used in putting up a building but will not do – wood, hay and stubble (1 Corinthians 3.12). Prophecy is not like that because it does the job properly. The Church built securely on the foundation of Christ will be strong and lasting through this gift.

b) *Prophecy encourages the Church*. The Greek word *paraclesis* reminds us of the title for the Holy Spirit in John's Gospel as the *Paraclete*. Literally, it describes the help that comes from one who stands alongside us in a time of trouble. A friend once passed on a card bearing a text to me at a time of great personal stress. With a mountain scene background it said 'If God is FOR US who can be against us?' (Romans 8.31). The sender of this card never knew of its relevance but the two simple words 'for us' took on prophetic force in those trying days. They reminded us of the presence of one by our side then and there in all the stresses which we were feeling, who would certainly bring us safely through.

c) *Prophecy comforts the Church* – The term here *paramythia* refers to the solace and calm which soothes away pain and hurt. The Church and Christian individuals are often in need of its application. It is through this ministry that the wounds which can fester, are healed. How can you comfort a man whose little child has just died, when his wife confesses to him at that moment that in fact he was not the child's father? I know of such excruciatingly painful experiences which God has miraculously healed through a prophetic word speaking hope and affirmation into the personal whirlpool of doubt and despair. As for individuals so for churches. These words go deeply beneath the surface to minister especial security from God to the distressed. Further to this in the same chapter v.24 Paul adds a fourth helpful effect.

d) *Prophecy convicts the unbeliever.* For it is a means by which his inner secrets are revealed. Christ speaks to him whilst the Church is worshipping with the gifts. I have known of this happening quite frequently. On occasions the unbeliever has been defensive about it, suspecting that someone has come along beforehand to 'spill the beans'. It is only when they realise that God has been speaking to them through prophecy that they appreciate that He does search them out. Then they turn to Him in faith, repentance and conversion with the conclusion 'God is really among you!' If they 'fall down and worship God' in the process, then here is one Scriptural passage which adequately explains the gesture we have already examined and found to be potentially misleading. Here however, the falling is almost certainly forward in prostration, not backwards in a swoon. No one is laying hands upon the person when it happens, but they are seeking God's mercy.

There are three similar modes of revelation to prophecy which we should include here. First, the *gift of tongues followed by interpretation*. Paul refers to this 'He who prophecies is greater than he who speaks in tongues unless he interprets' (1 Corinthians 14.5). 'For this reason he who speaks in a tongue should pray that he may interpret what he says' (1 Corinthians 14.13). The evidence suggests that tongue speaking was a frequent manifestation in the early Church. It has returned to the foreground in more recent years and again Scripture has positive statements to make about the value of the practice as part of our personal prayer life. Since it is prayer to God in the words of an unlearned language, there is a sense in which we express the deepest spiritual desires which would otherwise be inexpressible. Nevertheless, Paul is adamant on the need for interpretation in its public use. Given this also, tongues plus interpretation can become powerfully effective. On the day of Pentecost these twin gifts taken together rivetted the attention of a great crowd to Peter's inspired preaching of the Gospel. We had a similar occurrence in Streatham on a much smaller scale. A young Muslim man from Nigeria was friendly with an English girl and together they came to a prayer meeting. Someone spoke in tongues in the meeting and this young man identified the language as being that of a neighbouring tribe. He came to me afterwards to ask me to introduce him to his supposed compatriot. (I should add that he recognised the language but was not sufficiently proficient in it to be able to check the interpretation that was given.) When I told him that there was no one else from his homeland and then went on to explain the manifestation of tongues and further to speak of Christ to him he made a response to Christ there and then. Tongues with interpretation had been of value in introducing him to Christ.

Secondly, there are also *words of wisdom and knowledge*. Paul speaks about them in his list of gifts in 1 Corinthians 12.8 though there are no explicit scriptural examples given to put their nature beyond question. This biblical vagueness ought to make us somewhat wary of hard and fast definitions. Nonetheless we may safely assume that Jesus ministry of the gifts sets the standard for our own. When He demonstrates His personal insight into the lives of Peter, Nathaniel, the Samaritan women and numerous others, He shows how words of knowledge should work (John 1.42,47; 4.19). By this means God tells us facts about others which they may not know themselves or that they would not wish others to know. They need to receive them however, if they are to know God's blessing often expressed in physical healing. Words of wisdom are utterances which have unexpected wisdom in them, in that they apply an old truth in a new way. According to Arnold Bittlinger they are the words which resolve a difficulty or silence an opponent. Jesus' word about the tribute money is a good example (Luke 20.20–26). Yet we need to beware of over confidence. It soon leads to a departure from reality. I have heard very able Christians demonstrate their fallibility again and again in this way because it is the present fashion to minister healing on this basis. Such words may be nothing more than pious guess work. On occasions it is possible that the words may be psychicly communicated. When they are genuine revelations from the Holy Spirit they will have a much higher success rate, but will probably occur much less frequently than the times when it seems as if the speaker has swallowed all the contents of a mighty big medical dictionary.

God also speaks prophetically to His people through *visions and dreams*. The difference between them on the basis of the age of the recipient is fortunately not important. 'Young men . . . visions . . . old men . . . dreams', according to Joel, and quoted by Peter at Pentecost. By this process God implants His message visually in the mind of His servant. In the case of the vision, God's servant is physically conscious at the time. With the dream, the same thing happens but during a period of sleep when the mind is at rest. There are dozens of examples in the Bible. Father Abraham is the first to receive such a communication (Genesis 15.1). Prophets like Daniel describe them, and indeed interpret them in such detail that even Christians today still study his experiences (e.g. Daniel 7.15ff). That Jesus also was conscious of receiving special revelations from His Father in His baptism and also from the devil in the temptations which followed this is plain (Luke 3.21–4.12). At His transfiguration the experience was

remarkably strong (Luke 9.28). When His disciples returned
from their ministry He describes a similar perception (Luke
10.18). 'I saw Satan fall like lightning from heaven.' He
then has a clear assurance about His disciples: 'Full of joy
through the Holy Spirit, Jesus said "I thank you Father,
Lord of Heaven and earth because you have hidden these
things from the wise and learned and revealed them to little
children. Yes, Father for this was your good pleasure." '
Later there is also a profound awareness about future development to be fulfilled many years subsequently. 'When you
see Jerusalem surrounded by armies you will know that its
desolation is near' (Luke 21.20ff) From these experiences
of Jesus we can see that revelation received by vision is very
powerful. We have already mentioned the testimony of Paul
and God has many ways of getting through to us. The
major mark that this is what is happening is inward. For the
consequence is in the conscience and mind of the one to
whom God has spoken. Let Paul speak of this after his
Damascus road encounter with the risen Christ.

'When God who set me apart from birth and called me
by his grace was pleased to reveal his Son in me so that I
might preach him among the Gentiles, I did not consult any
man nor did I go up to Jerusalem to see those who were
apostles before I was, but I went immediately into Arabia
and later returned to Damascus' (Galatians 1.15–17). When
God has made such spiritual contact we are filled with the
awesome wonder of having dealings with Christ. The testimony of Jesus and to Jesus and from Him is the stuff of
which prophecy consists. The great desire of those who have
received such a revelation is that we might serve only Him.

How Revelations are Weighed

The first test must be to the witness of Scripture. Jonathan
Edwards was the founder of Princeton University but he
was also a mighty preacher in a time of great spiritual
awakening in New England, America in the 1740's. There
were as many outward signs of the activity of the Spirit in

his day as there are nowadays, but Edwards was not impressed. 'A work is not to be judged by any effects on the bodies of men, such as tears, tremblings, groans, loud utterances, agonies of body or the failing of bodily strength . . . because the Scripture nowhere gives us any such rule.' he declared. Among those who are being converted he adds that the genuine marks 'cause in man a greater regard to the Holy Scriptures, and establishes them now in that truth and divinity' (*A Narrative of Surprising Conversions* – Select Works). It is so for all who receive revelations from God. The Holy Spirit never contradicts this primary relevation then by secondary personal words. If the word or vision is from God it will also accord with the message of Scripture. Christ is the great theme of God's Word. Thus the test of the genuineness of this word is to the extent to which it exalts Him, honours Him and reflects Him. Words which appear to magnify other doctrines in such a way as to cast a shadow on Christ's primacy are shown to be false by this test. In this way we can perceive the falsehood of such prophetic words as those that major on the state of Israel today. It is not that Israel is of no significance to Christian people. The Bible indicates otherwise. But if the suggestion is that an Israeli citizen is better off in Jerusalem as an Israeli because of the richness of its association and traditions, than he could be in Christ as a believer, the word is wrong. It does not match up with the Bible's insistence that there is only one way to God – through Jesus.

A second test is resonance. Bruce Yocum uses this term which describes what happens if you ring a bell near another similar in size and shape. The vibration of the first causes a responsive ring in the second. So when the Spirit speaks through one there is a response in the hearts and spirits of the others who hear. It may not be with a total identity with the whole content of what is said but more with its tone and spirit. We will sense that it is right. It does not jar. It follows up previously known words. There is a harmony of direction about it and it feels good.

Thirdly, the fruit of the word is important. If it leads to criticism then it is probably false. If it promotes despair in the Church then again it is likely to be wrong. I was in a church recently when an excessively vague prophetic word was seized on by a member. 'That's the third time God has warned us like this', he declared. 'If we don't get things right now, we never will before Christ returns.' But the problem was that no one was at all sure of where it was that the Church had been so hopelessly wrong and so clearly warned. Personally I do not think that the Holy Spirit is quite as impatient with god's Church as we sometimes are. Genuine prophecies of warning usually include a gracious 'if' clause to show us the way out of the trouble we are facing.

If the word leads to the exaltation of its speaker more than to confidence in Christ it deserves to be forgotten. David Hill suggests that it was wrong motives combined with the absence of anything of religious or intellectual value that caused the decline into ineffectiveness of Montanism in the second century. This was an early Church revivalist movement headed by a gifted leader Montanus. One of the great Christian intellects of the day Tertullian identified with it himself late in his life. It could have had a much more significant effect for good in the Church. But two of its most prominent leaders Prisca and Maximilla lost their way. The movement died out and its Charismatic emphasis was soon overtaken by institutionalism. Like its successors Montanism was able to generate much genuine spirituality but it could not mature it. All present day Charismatic Church life needs other disciplines if it is to maintain its zeal and develop its potential and we will consider what these are later on.

Fourthly, predictive prophecies must be confirmed by fulfilment or partial fulfilment. In our early days in Scotland we had just such a personal word for the daughter of the local Pentecostal pastor. He was a member of a small Ministers Prayer Group and so told of the distress he and his wife felt for their girl Rosemary who was suffering deep depression following a bad bout of 'flu. The word for her was explicit. 'Tell Rosemary that a man will come from Hamilton and she must do whatever he tells her.' I don't know who was more surprised with this word, the speaker or Rosemary when she first heard it. Later on the same day the ring at their door revealed the gentleman from Hamilton who had arrived there and then to see her. He was a consultant psychiatrist to whom the family GP had spoken earlier in the day. He assured Rosemary that a little drug treatment was all that she needed in order to get better, and much to everyone's surprise and delight she accepted his advice and received the treatment. She was soon totally well again. The word to her was wonderfully complete – fulfilled in every detail. Yet she would never have felt able to receive advice from a psychiatrist without the word because of the suspicion with which they were regarded in the church by some of its members but not her father.

Fifthly, no-one can be an effective discerner of their own prophecies. Leaders, counsellors and ministers are helpful but the whole Body has a role here. Prophets are to offer their words to the Church in the context of their part in the life of the whole Body. Isolated prophets are in great danger of merely causing offence by a falsely superior attitude which enables them to distance themselves from the Church whilst they presume to speak to the Church about what it should become. On the contrary, the whole Church needs to weigh carefully what is being said if the words are to be of value.

Sixthly, the character of the prophet is important. 'For no good tree bears bad fruit, nor again does a bad tree bear good fruit for each tree is known by its own fruit' (Luke 6.43). It is not as if the gift of prophecy is a merit badge granted because of virtue. Nevertheless, if the prophet does not manifest the fruits of the Spirit as well as the gifts, how can we trust him?

Lastly, words from God often promote further refelection before we can understand them aright. When we listen for the voice of God we need to give Him time to speak. A

Benedictine Monk has written an excellent little pamphlet on this subject and he makes this point out of his own experience which I confirm out of mine. After praying about a certain matter I often find words and phrases coming to mind which seem to me to be the voice of God. Often the word is 'peace'. I know that this means that I need to rest where I am. On other occasions it may be 'go for it'. Praying about a new initiative in evangelism recently I felt this strongly and have since moved forward in pioneering ways with many confirmations that this is right. It is important to add that when we listen for the Lord's voice we are also most careful not to listen to Satan's subtle suggestions at the same time. It is here that the value of a true spiritual counsellor is invaluable. Share your convictions with one whom you trust. Allow him to speak honestly to you. Be willing to test out your hopes and fears in this way and you will be saved much possible harm.

Practical Requirements

In the receiving of a prophetic word for others we should notice that words are often only partially given first of all. It is the same with picture words or visions. This was our experience in the church once with a vision of a swan sailing down the middle of an attractive wide river. One described the scene in such vivid terms that we could easily picture it in our mind's eye. Then another took up the scene. The swan had its wings slightly raised like a sail and was being blown gently along. It spoke to us of all that was happening as the Spirit was moving in our midst. Then a third took up the same word. The swan had come to a place where the river had to pass through lock gates which were jammed shut. On the gates there was some graffiti and the first word was 'finance'. No more progress in the church until you get your money sorted out was the clear word. God spoke to us through this and the church received the word and acted on it to the great delight of the Treasurer and indeed all the fellowship.

There is a sliding scale principle in the weighing of these revelations. That is that words of little significance require little attention because they are soon forgotten. If they are more important it would be well for the leaders of the community to note them and decide an appropriate response. If they affect the whole Church or are of major importance then they need even more scrutiny by the whole Body. One of my friends always does me the kindness of giving me her words in writing. She is not able to get out to church as often as she might wish, but it does not stop her from hearing and transmitting a lively contribution to worship by this means. If the word is to direct the attention of the whole church to a new priority which they have not previously recognised we can be assured that God will confirm it many times by other means.

Methods by which we may do this could be as follows:

a) *Write down or record* all offerings as they are being given. A good shorthand writer is an invaluable asset. The word typed, filed, dated and with the circumstances briefly summarised is a great help.

b) *Discriminate the human factors*. Prophecy is an activity that is only partly inspired according to Paul (1 Corinthians 13.8). Slack speech, old world phraseology and repeated affirmations that 'this is really God speaking' are no help. The general rule is to dispose of as much of the human element as possible. When a little lady, unsympathetic with Mr Jim Callaghan's government declared that God was 'going to sock them up the bracket!' we knew what she meant without necessarily agreeing with the prophecy. It is true that Margaret Thatcher went on to win the next election but we did not attribute this to our little friend's prophetic accuracy!

c) *Get the word out of its metaphor*. If it is of God it should be understandable too. Many words need to be demythologised. I often précis an utterance in order to get at its meaning. 'Our friend is saying that God wants us to move forward in faith to a fresh stage in our mission', is a much more understandable statement than 'behold I have opened a great door of faith through which thou shouldest go in order to reach many multitudes . . .' It says the same thing but in a less involved way. The next stage after such a word is in prayer. 'Lord, what is this new step to which we should now come?'

d) *Test the word out on the basis of consistency* and common testimony. Genuine words are confirmed by other witnesses and the church, and they say 'it seemed good to the Holy Spirit and to us . . .' and act on that word.

Further Guidelines

Although there are difficulties ahead for the Church with the matter of prophetic words and the like, Scripture insists that we encourage the prophet not discourage him. 'Follow the way of love and earnestly desire spiritual gifts, especially prophecy', says Paul (1 Corinthians 14.1). And again 'Do not put out the Spirit's fire; do not treat prophecies with contempt. Trust everything. Hold on to the good' (1 Thessalonians 5.17). We must give room for prophetic ministries and stir up the gift in those who have received it. An atmosphere of love is essential if the gift is to flourish. We must be tolerant but firm. This means that we will encourage the more reliable prophets and do our best to discourage the unstable. When a brother from Cyprus arrived in the church once with the message that the Lord had sent him to exercise a teaching ministry in our midst, his loud Charismatic snortings in time of prayer were more than enough for most of the rest of us. I had no difficulty at all in telling him that if he was to come to us at all he would have to enter much more submissively before we could receive him. This was all too much for him however, so that he soon moved on elsewhere. Charismatic churches need the protection of firm leadership in these areas. Their warmth and openness make them very attractive to the unstable who always cause a great deal of trouble if their views are treated with indulgence. We are well advised to take the same view as is expressed in the *Didache*, a document of church orders from between AD70 and AD110. It says that like all travelling preachers prophets are to be received if their teaching agrees to that of the Church. But if a prophet (or an apostle) remains for three days and asks for money on leaving he is a false prophet. The marks of genuineness are financial disinterest, practical consistency and above all 'having the ways of the Lord.'

The major need for prophecy today is that it is to be *geared to a much larger agenda*. The little words tend to be too trivial for such a grand description. The larger words are still confined to safe options. For the most part they confirm the Church in its secure views and do not challenge us in the way of an Isaiah or Jeremiah in the Old Testament. Perhaps Martin Luther King, Dom. Helda Camara and Trevor Huddleston represent the kind of radical ministry for which prophets might begin to seek God and that the Church needs to receive. What a grand prospect there is for a church which dares to apply God's unchanging word to the deepest need of our race-torn, strife ridden and fear filled generation. There is no current renewal emphasis that is adequately facing this task. For larger revelations we need a larger Church. In Paul Tillich's words: 'The prophetic spirit has not disappeared from the earth. Decades before the world wars men judged the European civilisation and prophesied its end in speech and print. There are among us people like these. They are like the refined instruments which register the shaking of the earth on far removed sections of its surface. These people register the shaking of their civilisation, its self-destructive trends and its disintegration and fall decades before the final catastrophe occurs. They have an invisible and almost infallible censorium in their souls and they have an irresistible urge to pronounce what they have registered, perhaps against their own wills. For no true prophet has ever prophesied voluntarily. It has been forced upon him by a divine voice to which he has not been able to close his ears . . . Most human beings of course, are not able to stand the message of the shaking of the foundations. They reject and attack the prophetic minds, not because they really disagree with them because they sense the truth of their words and cannot receive it. They repress it into mockery or fury against those who know and dare to say that they know.' (*The Shaking of the Foundations* p.7–9).

All special revelations require special discernment too. The gift of prophecy is twinned with discernment in Paul's list in 1 Corinthians 12. We must not confuse our discernment with a mystical wisdom only open to the few who agree with us in every detail. Discernment involves judgment with a decision. It is not merely a surface opinion that will do. Such a response involves participation by the whole person – intellect as well as spirit. For the judgment to which we come will lead us to the deliberate choice of God's fresh way ahead. That leads to firm discipleship with greater obedience to Christ. It is to Christ the prophet that the spirits of all other prophets are always subject.

8

Discerning God's Will in Guidance

From His earliest days Jesus was increasingly aware of His special relationship with His Father. A vivid demonstration of this was in an incident which occurred when He was twelve years of age and had been to Jerusalem with His parents for the Passover celebration. At the end of the feast they started on the return journey home to Nazareth only to discover to their surprise that Jesus was not in the party with them. Hastily they retraced their steps the day's journey to the city, there to find Jesus in the temple courts engaged in earnest discussion with the teachers. His response to their rebuke must have puzzled them at least as much as it annoyed them and Mary did not forget it. 'Why are you searching for me?' said Jesus. 'Didn't you know that I had to be in my Father's house?' (Luke 2.49).

Since there is an exclusiveness in His Sonship there is a real sense in which no other can share in its immediacy. It is special to Him as God's 'one and only Son' (John 3.16). Clearly it is the source for His strength in times of temptation. It is the secret of His confidence in moments of personal inadequacy when He confesses 'The Son can do nothing by Himself, He can only do what He sees His Father doing' (John 5.19). It strengthens His resolve in the face of His impending cross. 'Now my heart is troubled and what shall I say? Father, save me from this hour? No, it was for this very reason I came to this hour. Father, glorify Your Name!' (John 12.27). It explains and enhances the value of His promise to all His disciples concerning the Holy Spirit. 'Do not leave Jerusalem but wait for the gift My Father promised which you have heard me speak about. For John baptised with water, but in a few days you will be baptised with the Holy Spirit' (Acts 1.45). We cannot understand the Gospel story at all without a grasp of Christ's relationship with the Father who sends both Him and the Spirit. The whole message of salvation to us is to do with coming to God the Father through the sacrificial offering made by God the Son and by the regenerating influence of God the Spirit. More than this, as we must go on to see, it sets out a sound theological framework on which our understanding of our own relationship with God may rest secure.

Whilst Christ's relationship with His Father is marked by uniqueness, it is also true that personal spiritual maturity never comes for us until we grow into a living experience of the relationship of sonship for ourselves. The purpose of all true faith is that we believe not only in Christ, but also in the Father who sent Him (John 12.44). Paul points out that access to the Father is the end to which both the work of the Son and the work of the Spirit are designed. 'Through Him we both have access in one Spirit to the Father' (Ephesians 2.18). As we begin to discover God as our Father the Holy Spirit authenticates our own sonship with God. As Paul says, 'By Him we cry Abba Father. The Spirit Himself testifies with our spirit that we are God's children' (Romans 8.15). The immediate consequence is clear. Through the leading of the Spirit God's guidance comes as a natural development releasing us from our fears and leading us on to God's glory. That is to say that getting to know the Will of God for our lives is a sure sign of being one of God's children. The more we are growing in spiritual maturity the clearer our understanding of His Will becomes. One of our most exciting discoveries is of the way in which God graciously overrules our mistakes and our sinful errors when we repent and turn to Him for forgiveness. There is a vastness and a goodness to His purposes for He can even turn our sins into good account.

We approach the practical issues of discernment in the Will of God therefore in a spirit of confidence and hope. For the mind of God is preoccupied by His thoughts concerning His people. This is the conviction of the psalmist. 'How precious *concerning* me are your thoughts O God! How vast is the sum of them! Were I to count them they would out-number the grains of sand' (Psalm 139.17–18). God's order embraces the universe though it is still in a state of dislocation through sin. Yet God has thought through a detailed plan for our lives even to the extent of the contents of our daily timetable. 'All the days ordained for me were written in your book before one of them came to be' (Psalm 139.16). How then do we discover His Will in major decisions but also in those which affect our more personal daily living.

Preliminaries for Guidance

In order to discover God's plan for our lives we need to take note of the mistaken notions that will often inhibit our progress if not adequately answered.

a) *Firstly, it is always wrong to stereotype the way in which God speaks to us since His methods vary.* I have already made the point about the use of Scripture as primary and normative. We have looked at prophecy, dreams and visions as special means of revelation which God can and does use from time to time. There are three other methods to add at this point. God frequently employs several within our experience as a sign of His merciful love.

When we are seeking God's Will it is good to take every opportunity we can get to listen to good expository preaching. In my experience there have been several occasions in which God has sorted out a personal problem for me in this way. From the testimonies I have heard from others, evidently He has also used my preaching from time to time, with this as the result for some of the hearers.

The late Dr Martyn Lloyd-Jones would never spend time counselling a confused member of his congregation at Westminster until after they had attended his services and listened to his preaching. Very often the confusions were dispelled through a sermon and the public counsel it contained adequately answered all the problems. It means that the number of people wanting to see him was much more manageable as a consequence. It leads to an effective and economic use of everybody's time. Sometimes He also speaks through personal conversations with a tested friend. Genuine friendships are a valuable acquisition and need to be zealously nurtured. According to Proverbs, whilst there are many who gather around in times of prosperity, 'there is a friend who sticks closer than a brother' (18.24). His relationship is marked by constancy even when he disagrees with us. 'Faithful are the wounds of a friend' (27.6). Christians who are bereft of friends are often at a loss in discovering God's Will. He is a friend indeed who can love us enough to admonish us when he sees that we are out of God's Will. If he can go further by opening his own heart to us in an attitude of equally trusting brotherhood, then he is a powerful mouthpiece through whom God can speak to our hearts. Often it is only the friendships which have stood the test of time that are like this. Never lose an old friendship in order to make a new one!

God's guidance may be circumstantial. It is unwise to take our circumstances as an invariable guide, since the devil can easily manipulate them in order to deceive the unwary. Just as he can also mis-apply Scripture to the same end. Yet circumstances are not irrelevant as the Scriptures plainly show. The case of the Church in China today is a good illustration of this. Many people prayed that Communism would never take control there when this became a distinct possibility from 1946 onwards. In fact, their prayers were not answered as they hoped, but we can now see that God has overruled the situation remarkably. Not only did the triumph of Communism lead to the release of many missionaries into the rest of South-East Asia for the strengthening of the Church there, but it has also lead to a vast spontaneous growth of the Church in China from some five million in 1948 to a conservatively estimated sixty million today. If God is guiding us by His power He may well overrule our prayers in any immediate situation, but we can also be sure that there will be some other signs confirming to us that this is indeed His purpose and we will come to some of them shortly.

b) *Never confuse God's Will with your own inclinations*. Most of us have grown up in a world which makes much of *success* as a suitable goal, and it is easily pressed into Christian service. It is a mistaken notion but it derived directly from Church growth teaching which can be very helpful in other respects. *Power* has a similar quality about it, especially in its Charismatic dimensions. *Ambition* directed to the great goal of pleasing ourselves through dominating others and manipulating circumstances makes its own appeal too. But we can be sure that God's purposes are never fulfilled in these ways. To indulge them says much more about us than it does about the Will of God and we need to be ruthless in crucifying such inward tendencies. We have the case of Saul in the Old Testament who abused his anointing and eventually lost it because he was addicted to pleasing himself. Simon the sorcerer was remarkably converted too, but we are told that he was willing to pay handsomely in cash, if only he could receive the power to bestow the Spirit on others. This wrong desire arising out of human pride only brought him condemnation since his heart was not right with God.

To follow our own inclinations in the place of God's purposes will always make us men-pleasers rather than God-seekers. It does not matter how much we attribute our motives to the Lord and His purposes, He always knows if our hearts are not clean before Him. Those whose motives are corrupted frequently change their friends and associates. They follow first this one and then the other, but it is for manipulative purposes. They are only using the friendship as a stepping stone for their own advancement. There is no

depth of interest there for they are on their way up! Having
employed the competitive attitude of the world in the cause
of the Kingdom they never seem to get any further on
spiritually. The reason is that it is only the pure in heart
who will see God, according to Jesus. Those whose motives
are mixed stand no chance of catching more than a glimpse
of the glory that passes.

Another consequence to this confusion is in the lack of
peace of those involved. In fact, it is the presence of God's
peace in our hearts that is one sure sign of being within the
Will of God. In the teaching of Jesus, peace is Christ's last
legacy to us. He said 'Peace I leave with you, My peace I
give you. I do not give to you as the world gives. Do not
let your hearts be troubled and do not be afraid' (John
14.27). Paul adds to that with his exhortation to 'Let peace
rule in your hearts since as members of one body you are
called to peace, and be thankful' (Colossians 3.15). The
verb 'to rule' here comes from the world of sport and can
be translated 'umpire'. If we have peace, we are in a
condition in which disharmony, stress and anxiety are ruled
out of court and we are in a composed state. As the umpire,
peace will not allow their presence. Misleading personal
prophecies are always revealed by this means. It does not
matter how convincing they may appear to be, if this is
their effect we need to renounce them immediately. Idle
daydreams about success or power or change will always
destroy our peace. They can never be confused with God's
Will since its characteristic qualities are so contrary. Instead
of producing a neurotic effect it is 'good, pleasing and
perfect' (Romans 12.2). Let the devil attempt to lead us
astray by a variety of subtle ploys. If God has implanted
His peace within us it acts as an inward censor by which we
can spot them and steer clear.

c) *Never claim infallibility for your own understanding
even when it is buttressed by firm convictions*. Infallibility is
a difficult notion to sustain because it is not within the range
of our abilities but only God's. There is no one individual
whose prophetic words have always been right because God

does not work in that way with human flesh. In my opinion, the more assertive a leader becomes on the strength of his supposed anointing, the more suspicious we should be about his motives. It is the same with groups of elders who share leadership in a church once they become directive over the lives of others.

We can keep a check on ourselves with these dangers by two means. Firstly, the application of personal humility works wonders. Such an attitude is much easier if it is adopted voluntarily. Peter urges us to this: 'Clothe yourself with humility towards one another, because God opposes the proud and gives grace to the humble. Humble yourselves therefore under God's mighty hand that He may lift you up in due time' (1 Peter 5.5–6). Secondly, the frank admission of past mistakes leading us to personal repentance. Far from this meaning the loss of our personal sense of anointing, it is the best means for increasing these things. It is an attitude of heart that is pleasing to God. It also keeps us approachable to others. My greatest heroes in the church have always been men who have recognised that they have feet of clay and have shared their weaknesses from time to time. I don't think that I am an exception in this. For it is one of the ways of showing that we are still involved in the learning process. If we are interested in discernment it is good to show that we understand how mistakes can and do happen, even with us.

Some Positive Principles

We have seen that a right relationship with God and with His people is a prerequisite for the discovery of His Will. It is the first part of every one of His plans for His own children. What are the hallmarks for which we should be looking as God continues to reveal His purposes to us?

a) *God's Will is characterised by consistency.* There will be a basic agreement between the new word God speaks and any guidance we have received thus far. Sadly, I have often come across those whose experience is a long chain of inconsistencies linked together by wasted opportunities. It may seem a sign of great spirituality for a young man to abandon his medical studies just before taking finals in order to join a team engaging in literature distribution in a developing country overseas, but I doubt it. If God has planned this, it is very unlikely that He will have ordered the previous five years of detailed and expensive study which is still incomplete. There is a logical development in the Will of God and often the best way of discovering what He is saying now concerning the future is to review what He has been saying previously over several months and years. Then we can hear the new word since it comes in the sequence of the revelations already received and we can follow it through to the next stage. This is not to say that God never causes a person to make a sudden change in his direction. There are, of course, exceptions and it does happen, but God's normal way with us is to take us right through the course of action until we have come to its appropriate conclusion. It is well worth the delay in the long run. Overseas eighteen years service from one who is fully qualified is much more likely to be blessed than twenty years from one who is still without professional commendation.

Having said this, God's Will is often only made clear to us when we are on the point of departure out of it. This is His promise according to Isaiah, 'Although the Lord gives you the bread of adversity and the water of affliction your teachers will be hidden no more; with your eyes you will see them. Whether you turn to the right or to the left your ear will hear a voice behind you saying, this is the way, walk in it' (Isaiah 30.20–21). When we were ministering in Scotland several years ago we felt as if we were on this unappetising diet described by Isaiah, and after about three years sought the opportunities to move south again. Nothing came of them however, and God sent a brother into our home with a clear prophetic word. 'Seven years here I think', he said, 'then you will move on.' Since his advice coincided with other bits of information we had received from elsewhere we settled down where we were for another four years. In the fulness of time we did move on. It was six years and eleven months after the beginning of the pastorate. It is an unkind reflection on the many good times we had to observe that we gained one month's remission for good conduct whilst north of the border. 'I being in the way the Lord leads me' is a poor translation of the Scripture verse, yet it contains a worthy truth. So long as we are moving within the Will of God where we are, the Lord's leading will be straightforward. If it is in a significantly new direction, again we need to look for other confirmations.

God's Will for us is always consistent with His own character. The outstanding qualities which are revealed to us in guidance are first His truthfulness. The strange Old Testament prophet Balaam is an outstanding example of one who discovered this. His story is recorded in Numbers 22–24. He lived in Pethor on the river Euphrates at the time when the children of Israel were travelling towards the river Jordan prior to their entry into Canaan near Jericho. His people were of the tribe of Moab who were lead by King Balak who had no desire to play host to Israel or even to have them as his next door neighbours. Balaam had already gained a reputation as a soothsaying prophet who could influence the future. So Balak sought his help, promising considerable financial rewards if only he could stop any further advance by Israel. A purse for a curse! It is then that we have the extraordinary incident with the donkey which contributes to Balaam's conclusion that he cannot comply with Balak's request. 'God is not a man that he should lie, nor the son of man that he should change his mind. Does he speak and then not act. Does he promise and not fulfill. I have received a command to bless, he has blessed and I cannot change it.' He goes on to say: 'The Lord their God is with them. God brought them out of Egypt . . . see what God has done.' God's Will is always consistent with His integrity.

b) *God also shows Himself to us as a gracious God*. Some may portray God as one with a malignant sense of humour given to outbursts of vindictive trantrums but this is a caricature of His quality of righteous anger. In fact, in His dealings with us, He is seldom provoked to respond in this way. 'The Lord is compassionate and gracious, slow to anger, abounding in love . . . He will not always accuse . . . He does not treat us as our sins deserve or repay us according to our iniquities. For as high as the heavens are above the earth, so great is His love for those who fear Him. As far as the east is from the west so far has He removed our transgressions from us' (Psalm 103.8ff). This quality of grace gives hope to the sinful man as it does to the errant Church. Avoid hasty words of judgment on the Church because of its failures leading to prophecies of its imminent doom. God is far more patient with us than we are with each other. He is also far less self seeking.

In guidance God comes to us as Saviour, Restorer and Keeper. He controls all the unknowns of the future and masterminds every detail of the present. His invitation to us is 'Call to me in the day of trouble, I will deliver you and you will honour' (Psalm 50.15). The personal testimony of the people of God throughout the ages is 'This poor man called and the Lord heard him, He saved him out of all his troubles' (Psalm 34.6).

c) *God's Will is always consistent with His international impartiality*. Our circumstances differ enormously and God's people are all individuals. He is prepared to put up with a wide variety of differences in His Church and shows little sign of standardising its outward forms. Nevertheless His dealings with us are common to all. 'God does not show favouritism and accepts men from every nation who fear Him and do what is right' (Acts 10.34–35). This is why the Gospel goes to all nations and the Church emerges in such kaleidoscopic variety. The same God and the same Gospel allows for this and is committed to producing this intensely interesting result. There are many other qualities in the character of God, but this is how He reveals Himself to those who are seeking His Will.

d) *God's Will is always communicated to us*. For our encouragement we are assured that God will begin to speak to us at the point where we are rather than at the point where we should be. It is important that we respond to what God is saying to us today. It is surely for this reason that we find the name of Rahab the prostitute included in the list of faith heroes in the Letter to the Hebrews (11.31). God spoke to her, and in spite of her sinful life she responded in faithful obedience, and so was spared when Jericho's inhabitants were killed.

It follows that the word God speaks to us will tell us as much about ourselves as it does about the Lord. If it is an injuction not to fear but to believe, then God is surely reminding us of our timidity. If He is speaking to us about healing our inner hurts then we are still inwardly sick. If He is encouraging us in faith then it is our tendency to draw back, which needs attention. If we are being warned of the dangerous consequences of disobedience, He is showing us how easily we have erred and strayed from His ways as with a lost sheep.

In His goodness God is prepared to accept our relative blindness in spiritual issues. He knows our condition, marred as it is by the effects of our sinfulness. There is an important equation to bear in mind in guidance. The more radical God's purpose for us is, the more frequently we may expect Him to speak to us about it. We should never embrace life changing plans if they have not been confirmed with increasingly detailed revelations about their contents. Abraham and Sarah's experience with their remarkable promise of a son and heir long after they had got beyond the normal age of child bearing is relevant. Firstly the promise was general that God would make them into a great nation which would bless all people (Genesis 12.3). Then it became more specific – that they would have a son of their own (15.3). Following this, the promise is defintely given to Sarah, causing Abraham some mirth (17.15). After this Abraham receives a visitation from the Lord Himself in the form of three human visitors with the same word – to be fulfilled in the next year (18.10). This time it is Sarah who cannot stifle her laughter as she has been listening in at the

door. At last God's Word is fulfilled. 'The Lord did for
Sarah what He had promised. Sarah became pregnant and
bore a son to Abraham in his old age, at the very time God
promised him. Abraham gave the name Isaac to the son
Sarah bore him' (21.1–2).

A Growing Relationship

When God takes us through this faith developing process it
is important to notice His method. Only occasionally do we
actually hear God speak to us with our physical ears. The
experience of hearing God may be vivid but most frequently
we hear God inwardly. 'The word is very near you; it is in
your mouth and in your heart so that you may obey it'
(Deuteronomy 30.14). Sometimes we have it in our hearts
long before we are prepared to admit it. It is when we come
to the point of confession that everything falls into its place,
and the message is duly received. It is the same in our
experience as it is in the whole process of creation. God's
uttered word becomes the means for its own fulfilment. Paul
reminds us that it is like this with salvation. 'If you confess
with your mouth "Jesus is Lord" and believe in your heart
that God raised Him from the dead you will be saved'
(Romans 10.8–9). Hence the first question to someone who
is struggling with the Will of God for their lives is always
this. 'What do you think God has already said to you about
this?' As we hear their response, we can form an opinion
on the reliability of their conviction in the matter. If they
have no inward conviction, it is probable that they still have
not yet heard God speak on the matter at all.

Objective Signs

There are immediate consequences of hearing God speak.
Jesus indicates three in His well loved teaching of the
Shepherd and the sheep.

a) *As His sheep we immediately begin to follow Christ*
(John 10.4). We are attracted and held by the tones of the

voice which we recognise. Christ Himself is our Master and none other. Since Christ's picture is drawn from the east, He does not drive us out before Him, but He leads His sheep. We know He is always a little ahead of us, calling us forward by name, assuring us of the way ahead which He is still opening up on our behalf. One of the purposes of praying is to let Him know that we are still within following distance.

b) *At the same time, we are fleeing from the voice of a stranger's whom we do not recognise* (John 10.5). In the process of discerning God's Will there is the need for rejection as well as submission. Since His disciples did not immediately understand this point Jesus goes on to describe the strangers whom we should avoid. They are the thieves and robbers who have an ulterior motive in their pastoral concerns. They may be hired hands who do not really care much about the sheep. So long as their own pockets are well lined they never stay to protect their charges when a wolf enters the sheepfold. Behind these sinister figures there lurks an even more formidable foe in Satan himself. To perceive God's purposes it is essential that we repudiate his. This resistance of the devil and all his works is an immediate consequence to the discovery of our place in God's plans.

c) *As His sheep, we are also beginning to join in the most enriching fellowship with others here and now* (John 10.16). Christ's ultimate purpose for His own people is their unity in Him. He is also committed to this at this present time. So He is in the process of finding His sheep from a variety of backgrounds. 'Them also I must bring', He says. 'They too will listen to my voice and there shall be one flock and one shepherd.' The pastoral responsibility for the flock of God is Christ's. The diversity within it is ours to enjoy since God wants us to share in the pleasure of it. We must return to this point later as we consider the true Church of Christ today.

Some Golden Rules for Guidance

In pursuing the Will of God we must always allow for *the timing element*. The early Church had great difficulty with Christ's promises about His return for this reason. Peter tells us that this caused many to scoff at the promises and turn away from their Christian discipleship too. He goes on to say 'But do not forget this one thing dear friends: With the Lord a day is like a thousand years and a thousand years are like a day' (2 Peter 3.8). Many of us make a similar mistake to this over more personal issues. God will never be rushed. Yet once He begins to move, everything falls into place with astonishing speed.

Faith and persistence are always important. To fulfil the purposes of God we need to hold to the vision He has given us, especially when things are difficult. Every fresh venture of faith is always contested. There are always many more reasons for not going on with God's purposes at such times. These are sent to try out our convictions. If God has spoken to us however, we will not desist for this reason.

Unconfessed sin interrupts God's direction. To sin is to fall short of God's standards which are set for us in Christ. If we have not been aware of our failure at the time, then the Holy Spirit will sensitise our conscience about it before long. We need to repent of our sins and seek God's forgiveness. Very often God will bring us back to the very place where we were before we strayed. As we turn to Him again in prayer and contrition, so He begins to lead us forward.

Further revelation then becomes dependent on our present obedience. It is true that sometimes we are lead into following God for what appear to be flimsy reasons but they are nonetheless implanted by Him. I talked recently with a Christian leader who had found himself fulfilling a preaching engagement which he would not normally have taken in this way. Yet God used it to bring singular blessing to the churches involved. The extent to which we are prepared to follow Him will determine what He will now entrust us with. But no major decision should be undertaken on unsubstantiated evidence. If our plans are scripturally sound and appropriate to the circumstances, and approved by trustworthy colleagues then we should go right ahead with them no matter how much it costs. We never avoid the element of risk when we are discerning and following the leading of God. That is what makes it such an exciting activity. True discernment will lead us to the correct judgments in the light of this, and to the seizing of opportunities while they last.

9

Discerning Christ's Church

Christ came in order to build His Church. Although we only have two instances of His teaching in the matter, both of them make this unequivocally clear. They are recorded in Matthew's Gospel. The first in Peter's forthright confession at Caesarea Philippi (Matthew 16.13–20). To the direct question from Jesus 'What about you . . . who do you say I am?' Simon Peter blurts out the response which inaugurates the age of the Church as a unique new society. Jesus is not John the Baptist, Elijah, Jeremiah or one of the other prophets as others say. 'You are the Christ, the Son of the living God', Peter declares. Moreover, he perceived this vital truth in the way in which the Church is to grow in its understanding of the things of God. 'This was not revealed to you by man but by My Father in Heaven', says Jesus. His next words are a fine example of a play on words and have stimulated considerable commentary ever since. 'And I tell you that you are Peter, and on this rock I will build My Church, and the gates of Hades *will not prove stronger than it.*' In Aramaic, the language of ordinary speech at the time, one word *kepha* may be translated both as Peter and rock. For Christ builds His Church out of such human material as an obedient and faithful Peter. At this point Jesus adds the word about authority in ministry which is later addressed to the whole *ecclesia* (Matthew 18.18). 'I will give you the keys of the Kingdom of Heaven; whatever you bind on earth will be bound in heaven, and whatever you loose on earth will be loosed in heaven.' The keys of the Kingdom in the custody of the Church are the keys of insight more than the keys of administration, through which all others will be either admitted or excluded from God's Kingdom. The task of the Church is therefore to do with our theme of discernment. Which actions does the Church permit and which prohibit? On what grounds are people received or rejected? What about our words, our teaching and our attitudes? How does the Church come to its decisions?

The second word probably given in Capernaum again emphasises this paradox of uniqueness yet servanthood (Matthew 18.15–19). Since the Church is a company of sinful people intent on discovering more of the grace of God its special genius is in the area of relationships. Within its fellowship it is anticipated that the occasions will arise when its members will show their human frailty by sinning against each other. But the Church is made up of those who have come to a commitment of faith about a Christ who forgives and a Father who cares because the members of the Church have experienced God's grace for themselves. Hence it is composed of the forgiven and also more significantly the forgiving. When we are the victims of personal assault from fellow Christians Christ teaches us that there are four important responses to be made. Firstly, we are to seek to win back the offending brother by showing him his fault privately. Secondly, if this is ineffective, we are to underline the seriousness of his actions by showing him that he has a case to answer. There should be two or three witnesses to it who can vouch for the genuineness of the charge. Thirdly, if this again fails, the Church is to be involved and to pass judgment, not so much with a view to securing the conviction of the accused but in order to bring them to repentance and reconciliation. Only if this fails are we to come to the last point of separation from him. 'If he refuses to listen even to the Church, treat him as you would a pagan or a tax collector' (Matthew 18.17). He is no longer regarded as a member of the family but as a stranger who has yet to make his first discovery of what God's grace really means. Not that even this is the end of the matter. For Jesus goes on to apply the principle of spiritual authority already first given at Caesarea Philippi. The Church may restrict others or the Church may release others by its obedience to the commission to preach the Gospel. Furthermore, the Church possesses special authority in prayer. 'If two of you on earth agree about anything you ask for, it will be done for you by My Father in Heaven. For where two or three come together in My Name, there am I with them.' In the parable that follows it is evident that the thought of reconciliation through a freely granted forgiveness is still uppermost.

The uniqueness of the Church then is in its special discovery of the saving power of Christ, the Son of the living God. Its servanthood is in the fact that all its life and ministry, intercession and discipline is directed to the end that others might experience forgiveness for themselves.

Every ecclesiastical system which loses its sense of servanthood to the Gospel soon falls into a process of corruption and decay. It is only a servant Church that will grow to full maturity and thus discover its final destiny. God is on the look out for communities that are deeply rooted in the dynamics of forgiveness. Our quest in this chapter is the priorities for their life.

All this is made more important since a recovery of the doctrine of the Church as Christ's Body is the most vital characteristic of the present renewal. The truths of the Person of the Holy Spirit and of spiritual gifts had been the common property of the Church since the rise of Pentecostalism at the beginning of the twentieth century. With this emphasis within the Church of fresh renewal three conflicting ideas have emerged. They serve to underline the greater need for discernment.

a) *Charismatic denominationalists* see their task as one of effective witness within their own church structures so that they can win them over to a fresh openness and freedom to the Holy Spirit. Under good leadership an organisation like the Fountain Trust which took this view had commended itself to the leaders of the major denominations in the United Kingdom until its closure in 1981. Since then the level of confidence about it is probably much lower now than it was a decade ago.

b) *Sectarian Restorationists strongly oppose this hope.* For them there is no point in attempting the process of denominational renewal since the day for all denominations is now past and God is not in the business of renewing them. Those who take this view urge us to abandon these old structures in order to form new relationships which will more than replace the old. To the charge that this policy only serves to split the Church yet again in such a way that will inevitably lead to yet another denomination they respond with the conviction that we are living in the end times. Moreover, they think their church marks the final division between themselves and the apostate church beyond recovery.

c) I do not accept either of these propositions. In this chapter I am arguing for radical provisionalism. The basis is an acceptance of the Church as it is, and also the processes of history through which the Church has come to us. Added to this is the conviction that the society for which Christ died is not to be divided ecclesiastically, nor corrupted morally, nor haemorrhaged doctrinally, nor weakened into lifelessness spiritually. So the first task of the present day Church is to rediscover its roots. In turn this will lead us to the conviction of provisionality written into every expression of the Church at this present time, with hope. P. T. Forsyth expresses this well. 'I believe that the Church is the greatest and finest product of human history. It is the greatest thing in the universe because it is the product of the Holy Spirit in history.' Significant as our renewal insights on the Church are, I do not believe that the Church will discover all this merely by embracing these fresh understandings. But it will happen as the whole Church gives itself increasingly to the implications of the Scriptures about its life, health and ministry, without fear about the necessary changes such a commitment will bring.

The Scriptural Roots

The New Testament knows nothing of the isolated Christian who is apart from Christ's Church. The focus is always on the corporate Christian. The Church is God's *ecclesia*. This special term was used in a secular way of people summoned together by a herald. It has links with the Old Testament where the Lord's people are sometimes described as God's congregation or assembly (Numbers 23.2; Acts 7.38). But in the New Testament it is used to describe the new society God has wonderfully called together through Christ, to which a host of metaphors now apply. The Church is His Body, Family, Bride, Temple, Army and People, for the Church is always God's called out people assembling together in Christ's Name. Salvation is into the Church from the day of Pentecost onwards (Acts 2.37–47), the gifts of the Spirit exercised in the context of the Church (1 Corinthians 12.7). The process of personal sanctification and regeneration is also within the ambit of our membership of the people 'who were not a people but are now God's people' (1 Peter 3.9). The purpose of our individual experience is not merely our own salvation but the salvation of that of the whole Body. The Church expresses the experience of its members. It is the necessary outgrowth and development of regeneration. As individual Christians testify to 'a new birth into a lively hope through the resurrection of Jesus Christ from the dead and into an inheritance that can never spoil or fade' (1 Peter 1.3–4) so too does the Church. All its ministry is performed through the power of the Holy Spirit (Galatians 3.2–5). Its first leaders are primarily miracle workers rather than administrators (Luke 9.1; 10.1). Administration is not to be despised for it is a spiritual gift. (1 Corinthians 12.28). The essential message of the Church is that since Christ is alive and well, the Church can now do anything that He wishes His Church to do, by means of the gift of the Spirit. The Church can also do all these things now immediately providing they are within Christ's purpose and subject to His character.

There are but two presentations of the Church in the Scriptures. It is never seen territorially or denominationally, but either locally or universally. This indicates that the chief issue before all churches is never to do with their history or tradition but always to do with their true spiritual identity. Is the Church living in the good of its incredible heavenly resources in Christ? (Ephesians 1.20–22). Do we see ourselves as members of 'the Church of the firstborn whose names are written in heaven' (Hebrews 12.23). Or are we losing these glorious claims for the Church by our ignorance, sloth, unbelief or complacency? The greatest weakness of the Church is in her inability to believe God for all that is necessary for our life and strength. The Scriptures are indicating an inexhaustible supply of spiritual power, available to all Churches which will receive them. Those that do so flourish. Those that fail to do so through unbelief, disobedience or sin, wither and eventually die. From the letters to the Churches in the book of Revelation (chapters 2–3), we can see Christ's diagnosis of the sick Church. Spiritual sickness is never induced by adverse external circumstances but always through an internal condition brought about by our spiritual unresponsiveness.

In the Scriptures there is no necessary uniform organisation between churches. The assumption is that local churches are capable of sustaining their own life whether they are in Galatia (1 Corinthians 16.9), Macedonia (2 Corinthians 8.1) or Judea (Galatians 1.22). They are bound together through a network of relationships and sustained both by the local ministries of elders and also through the travelling ministries of evangelists, apostles and prophets. Local churches are always being urged into maturity. This is the point of Paul's prayer for the Ephesian Church (Ephesians 1.15–23, 3.14–20). The Church needs wisdom and revelation in order to understand all that Christ has for it. It is always infinitely more than the Church imagines. Paul's understanding brings him to the point of his application. 'I urge you to live a life worthy of the calling you have received' (Ephesians 4.1). It is as if he is claiming that there is nothing the Church cannot become since there is nothing that Christ cannot do for it. Paul's fine statements about the Church as the outward expression of Christ's present life brings us back to Christ's inaugurating words about the Church with which we begun. It is a church which is confessing Christ theologically and practically that is the genuine article. If we have been misled into a church which maintains a certain existence whilst it is divorced from its head, then we have linked to a fellowship in danger of imminent collapse. 'The mistake of ecclesiasticism has been to believe in the Church as a thing in itself', Archbishop Michael Ramsey remarked wisely. The Church is not a thing in itself or an end in itself according to the Scriptures. It is a gathering of Christ's people in the Holy Spirit with the sacraments and under Scripture. Christ is its source, purpose and end. There was scarcely a day when it was more necessary for us to examine the scriptural foundations of the Church in order to clarify our present credentials in the Body of Christ.

Present Responsibilities

Having urged the need to return to scriptural roots and patterns for the life of the Church, I need to call attention to the proper place of Scriptures for the present experience of the Church. They are to be seen as normative in that the Scriptures set the standards and priorities without being exhaustively descriptive of every detail of their own experience or ours. The Scriptures themselves accept the process of history which must not be neglected when we study them for our own doctrinal purposes. They teach a teleological, not a cyclical programme for the Church because they are always moving the people of God onwards from a known beginning to an end which is only partially revealed by them. Instead of presenting us with definitive directions they are the source book for every dream of how the Church is to become. Thus they do not support the notion that we must at all costs return to the Church of the New Testament in order to prove our orthodoxy. That cannot be done.

There are many New Testament churches anyway and which one do we choose as our model – Jerusalem, Antioch, Rome or Corinth or another? The Scriptures do not impose necessary restrictions on the organised expressions of the Church in which we find ourselves for geographical or denominational or personal reasons. Rather, they set the great principles by which all churches must test themselves. Every aspect of the Church's teaching and of its relationships are to be permeated by Scripture and tested by this means. For the Scriptures stimulate the life and judgment through which the Church enjoys the dynamism of the Spirit. We must attend to three Scriptural priorities if we are to experience this fully for ourselves.

a) *Headship*. The truth implicit in all our intercessions for the Church is that it does not belong to its members, ministers or benefactors, but to God and Christ. Paul's affirmation still rings true concerning the whole of His Church. 'Christ is the image of the invisible God the firstborn of all creation, for whom all things were created . . . and he is the head of the Body the Church, he is the beginning and the firstborn from the dead, so that in everything he might have the supremacy' (Colossians 1.15–18). It is in this context that we can understand the significance of the ministry of the Holy Spirit. Christ is the Head and the Holy Spirit is God at present active in God's Church, enabling the Church to do God's Will. That is why Christ concentrates His teaching to His disciples on the subject of the Spirit just prior to the cross. In John's Gospel this theme emerges clearly from chapters 14–16. The Holy Spirit will be with us for ever (14.16–17). He will teach us both by revelation and also recollection – stirring our minds to remember the teaching we thought we had forgotten (14.25). The Holy Spirit will bear witness to Christ (15.26–27). He will bring the ungodly world into a state of spiritual conviction on account of its sin. Christ's righteousness and God's judgment on evil (John 16.8–11). The Holy Spirit will have a ministry similar to that of the floodlight on a building of outstanding beauty or interest. 'He will not speak on his own – He will bring glory to me' (John 16.14).

Given that Christ is the Head of the Church the Holy Spirit gladly functions within. God's first words to church leaders is to call us back from our own false assumptions about our own responsibility or our own position. We are not to act as if the Church belongs to us when manifestly it belongs only to Him. Clearly, the Holy Spirit will always guide the Church whenever He is given the opportunity to do so. He often speaks in times of worship (Acts 13.1–4). He will inspire by direct vision (Acts 16.9) He will use the counsel of wise friends. He gives us a Word which is detectable because of its own inner witness to our own spirit.

In the light of this it is important that the leaders of the Church are those who are anointed by the Lord and then appointed by His people rather than those who are appointed by the church with the hope that maybe God's anointing will rest upon them. The sign of anointing is realistic response to Christ expressed through effective service. Anointed preaching, like anointed service, gets results. Happy the church whose leaders are capable of admitting their mistakes and jettisoning their own plans in favour of God's Will that has become more clearly known subsequently. To keep a leadership healthy there needs to be a balance of functions within it with the recognition that he who leads in one respect will not lead in others. Anointing is never necessarily in equal measure, but a plurality in leadership does not necessarily indicate equality. The truth of the matter is that we have not handled the Church of God well in our own day, often stifling what we should be stimulating and then releasing what we should bind. No wonder then that Christ's word to His Church today is 'that He wants His Church back.' Realistic renewal for the Church begins when its leaders gladly respond to His request.

b) *Membership*. The quality of the life of the Church is expressed by the relationships of those who are its members. This simple fact is so significant and yet so easily overlooked.

Whilst the great discovery of the Charismatic renewal has been that the Church is the Body of Christ, the most frequently used metaphor for the Church in the New Testament is that of the family in which mutual relationships are the primary quality. More than this, the relationship is that of the brothers and sisters sharing a common parentage not husbands and wives within a marriage contract. There is therefore no exchange of status in prospect nor any possible termination by way of the divorce courts because compatability is not always easy. We may notice the following characteristics in the bond between us.

i) It takes root best in the soil of weakness combined with grace. We will always find it hard to share our inner selves with those who choose to project themselves as paragons of virtue since such people are always somewhat threatening. Paul was never too high and mighty to hide his 'weakness, fear and much trembling' (1 Corinthians 2.3). We will build most constructively with others when we cease to manipulate them and freely admit to our own needs.

ii) It is expressed through intimate and tender care for each other. I will return to this a little further on, when considering the urgent dynamics for the Church which accepts the process of change that God has in store. Suffice to notice at this point that Christ's priority for His disciples still applies. 'A new commandment I give you: Love one another as I have loved you, so you must love one another. All men will know that you are my disciples if you love one another' (John 13.34). This is not a call to a love which is sensually indulgent, but to a love which is personally costly. There is a cross at its centre, because Christ alone is its model. It holds all who are Christ's within the warmth of its embrace.

iii) It sees the value of each individual, allowing them the dignity of their place in the Body of Christ and that of hearing God for themselves without another's necessary interruption into their lives. Every form of authoritarianism fails at this point. When Charismatics go in for their own expression of this through the evolution of omnipotent elderships and omniscient apostles – who incidentally are frequently falling out with each other – they devalue our individuality and deny the whole genius of renewal.

It is sufficiently strong to hold us unconditionally secure within the family of God even when we have obviously failed. Where the Church of God is living like this there will be many practical consequences. The Church will see that however impressive a large congregation may be, nonetheless small is also beautiful. Robert Banks has shown us that the maximum number that could reasonably be expected in the churches of the New Testament era would never have been more than forty to forty-five at the most. They met in homes which could not accommodate more than this in their largest room. It was not until the third century that we have evidence of special buildings being constructed to house Christian congregations. So the normal would be a small gathering. It would be one in which it is possible to exercise much healing since this is always a priority ministry in the church. I have already made the point that local churches are by far the best locations for healing ministries for other reasons. Since we seldom receive all the healing we need in one go, the need for regular ministry in this area is so much the greater. We need to see that since membership has to do with our part in Christ's community it is only a reality in as much as we fulfil, express and communicate the life of Christ's Body to others within Christ's Body by this means. The significance of membership to the church is functional. Names on rolls or in registers may be an administrative necessity but they are never to be confused with the spiritual intention.

c) *Church Discipline*. As we have already seen the Church of Christ is a forgiving community because it is a forgiven community. Discipline is not considered as the opposite of forgiveness as if it was simply an unkind demonstration of rigour. It is a strong and positive expression of the grace of forgiveness since its purpose is always restorative. The disciplined are those who are enabled and equipped to serve the Lord more adequately than they ever have previously, because others have cared enough for them to leave them to put away their sin. But discipline also links with discipleship. It is more than a matter of dealing effectively with our own personal tendencies to sinfulness, it has to do with a communal commitment to radical service. Having seen the shallow individualism which has character- ised much easy believism in the past it is important that we do not opt for a cosy Charismaticism which is equally self- centred in its concerns. Discipleship treats sinfulness seri- ously. Whilst God in Christ has met us with the offer of the Gospel which is sheer grace, yet there are discernible qualities which show whether in fact we truly receive God's grace in faith. The first is *metanoia* – repentance. It is a profound change of mind leading to a change of direction. It is a mistake to imagine that this can be produced by scolding congregations with a view to inducing a sense of guilt. It is the goodness of God which leads to repentance (Romans 2.21). The regrettable truth is that we sometimes enjoy a sense of guilt because it confirms us into a state of helpless inactivity. This, however, is nothing more than emotional torpor which is sometimes an easier option than the right response for which God is looking. Repentance calls for positive action in leaving our sin and following God and therefore it always links with faith. If we are taking our discipleship seriously, we will renounce the sins of the religious life as well as those of the fleshly life. Pride, envy and hypocrisy can be as devastating as wine, women and song and can only be dealt with by drastic action.

Our communal discipleship calls us into warfare of a sterner kind. The interest of the Church has been stirred by the recognition of the demonic in recent years and the practice of the explusion of demons on which I have already commented. We now need to see that the powers of evil are more than the personal demons of the Gospel. They are also the principalities and the powers which manifest themselves in society and in all of its systems. As God's alternative society the Church is called into conflict with the powers at every level. They are expressed by fear, hatred, oppression and destruction. They stir up the worst human responses in the most complex political, economic and even ecclesiastical and social structures. They always create a paralysis of nerve, a fear of man and a hatred of others. Racism, militarism, nationalism and acquisitiveness are their most prominent forms in today's world. Yet the Gospel word on the powers is that Christ is their victor. More than this, they are to be redeemed and the Church is God's disciplined instrument to that end. In contrast to their strength, which depends upon the power of illusion, Christ has all power and authority to deal with them. When His love, faith, acceptance and sacrifice are received and employed, then the powers are vanquished in Christ's Name. It is the calling of the Church to demonstrate this.

Dynamics for Change

Having considered our roots and responsibilities it is important to conclude with a summary of the qualities which I believe will rescue the Church from its present dangers and divisions and release it into God's much more abundant promises for the future. The assumption must be that there is a commitment to the process of change according to the Scriptures. There is no reason why any church should not enjoy God's convenanted benefits which always follow our obedience. Whenever there is this obedience then we will discern these qualities which will lead to a healthy community in Christ. To join with such a body would do us all the good in God's world, for such a Church will always be God's effective servant. If relationships within the Body are sound and the doctrine is clearly scriptural, the structures of the Church are secondary in significance. The problem facing the new separatists of the Restoration Movement is that of putting such an emphasis on the structures that they are falling into the trap of history. Inevitably they are already losing their hold on the priorities for a sound spiritual life. However, they are not alone in this. In order to move to a greater destiny the Church needs the following more attractive goals.

a) *A fresh Baptism of Love*. Love is the authentic hallmark of the Christian faith and its objective is the Lord Jesus Christ. As the New Testament frequently declares He has initiated the love bond. 'Christ loved the Church and gave himself up for her' (Ephesians 5.25). 'We love because he first loved us' (1 John 4.19). He nourishes and cherishes the Church out of His love. Having redeemed us from our sins through His love, He also sanctifies us through His love which is the root and ground of all of our being. Our developing Christian experience is an increasing adventure in the wide dimensions of the love of Christ. A sign of some maturity is when we know this love for ourselves and yet simultaneously confess that it is impossible to know all of this love. Paul's prayer for the whole of Christ's family expresses this. 'I pray that you may have the power together with all the saints to grasp how wide and long and high and deep is the love of Christ, and to know this love which surpasses knowledge' (Ephesians 3.17–18). We are to be locked into a love relationship with Christ. The Church cannot expect courageous developments without receiving and sharing much more of Christ's tenderness.

The test of having received this love is always practical. For it is those who know love who have the capacity to extend it to others. It is important that Christians should love the world in the same way that God does. It is also necessary for us to foster a love relationship within the Church of Christ, especially for those parts of it which were formerly outside the orbit of our own experience, and nevertheless within the faith of Christ. The ethos of our relationship must be that of a loving care for one another which seeks and grants forgiveness whenever it is needed. The whole of the Church is Christ's family, and to embrace the love of Christ will mean to stimulate acceptance, and expectation of one another. Narrow legalism in all its forms will be out. Dead nominalism and arid intellectualism also. Such a release of love as this is capable of producing much

healing within the Body. My own life was greatly transformed by the experience of a remarkable quality of love
from members of the Roman Church with whom I still have
profound theological differences. It was by revelation that
I came to a warm appreciation of the sacrifice, dedication
and commitment that characterises many in that Church
who regard themselves as blessed by Christ's sacraments
without necessarily being awakened yet by His Gospel.
Perhaps the need to demonstrate a similar quality of affectionate regard for our own immediate church family is the
more difficult expression for some of us. For it is almost an
article of faith to be most critical of those to whom we are
closest, who can also see all our faults. But a fresh affusion
of love will cover a multitude of sins. It will also create an
atmosphere of trust in which defensiveness is no longer
necessary and changes can be welcomed.

b) *The Quest for Spirit led Unity*. Christ's true Church
cannot be satisfied with its divisions. It is open to the
insistent pressure for unity from Scripture. Three passages
are enough to demonstrate this. In John 10.16–17 under the
analogy of the shepherd and the sheep Jesus insists that He
will bring us into one flock under His own shepherding care.
The flock will be characterised by one quality, that of loyalty
to the shepherd. In John 17.20–23 Christ prays for the same
thing. His people are to be in full organic unity with Him
and also with one another. As their unity is complete, so
the world will come to know Christ's love. In Ephesians
4.3,13 it is the unity which is in the Spirit of God's gift, which
precedes the unity in faith which we are yet to achieve, and
which is the logical outcome of unity in the Spirit.

If we are to find this unity we will need to co-operate
with all that the Spirit is doing to bring this about. He has
been using two major movements in recent years. First, the
worldwide Ecumenical Movement which began under the
impetus of world mission. One of its visionaries was William
Carey who proposed a great all denominational missionary
conference to take place in 1810 at the Cape of Good Hope.
This did not happen then, but the seed was sown for the

conference in Edinburgh which took place 100 years later, which took as its goal 'the evangelisation of the world in this generation.' The growing Churches of the Third World are heavily committed to ecumenism and they present the unanswerable case of one world with one Church.

The second major activity of the Spirit has been the renewal to which I have already referred. Its beginnings were in Pentecostalism at the turn of the century, but it has spread to all the Protestant denominations and also into Catholic and Orthodox Churches. For reasons already given, this renewal is not strong enough when it is separated from the doctrines and disciplines that come from the churches established traditions. Yet given these, there is an impetus for unity from this source which is uniquely helpful. There are all too many instances in what has begun in the power of the Spirit has ended up with fleshly displays of further fragmentation which are grievous. Nonetheless, by this means the Spirit is creating a fresh unity which is more colourful than we have ever known before in which the whole Church has a part.

c) *Commitment to New Strategies in Mission.* Christ's true Church sees mission as the natural expression of its faith. In the UK it is estimated that only a possible eleven million out of the total population of fifty-six million have any formal commitment to the Church. It is probable that three-quarters of the remaining number are beyond the traditional methods of evangelistic outreach. There is therefore no lack of opportunity for the Church to experiment in the fulfilment of its mission.

In addressing ourselves in this task we must expect many fresh initiatives to emerge. We are discovering the impact value of praise and celebration as the appropriate setting for making Christ known. There is immense potential in the use of small groups in evangelism. Drama and the arts may be used to portray and illustrate the message. The sacrament of baptism marking our entry into the new life of Christ is always powerful. Similarly, communion as Christ's love gift to the Church through which we may feed on Him in faith,

is profoundly challenging. The use of spiritual gifts and the
expectation of the presence of the Spirit through a ministry
of signs and wonders in healing will always provoke a
response.

Yet at the heart of our mission there is a great simplicity.
We are charged to declare the message of Christ and to
seek the verdict of faith in Him from those who hear our
message. For the most part it is not that people have
rejected Christ. As yet the vast majority have still not heard
of Him. There is indeed a profound spiritual enquiry after
Him at this time. As Christ's Church therefore gives itself
to the task of making Christ known it is probable that the
Church will lead others to Him and also find Christ for
themselves. Where there is an authentic evangelistic desire
in the Church the truth is plain. We have come across
another genuine member of His one family. Though those
who share in the family of God are similar they are never
dull. There is enough difference to make them interesting
and yet there are also these unmistakeable common characteristics revealing our shared heritage and destiny.

d) *Commitment to the Pilgrimage of Hope*. For the true
Church of Christ takes the scriptural promises for its future
seriously. We know we are sharing in Christ's family when
dissatisfaction with the church as it is gives birth to the
desire to change it, rather than encouragement to leave it.
Paul says 'Christ loved the Church and gave himself up for
her to make her holy, cleansing her by the washing with
water through the word, to present her to himself as a
radiant Church without stain, or wrinkle or any other
blemish but holy and blameless' (Ephesians 5.25–27). Those
who share in Christ's life, His love and His light, are always
certain to share in His wonderful transformations. The true
Church does not fear this. Indeed, we can discern the true
Church by its capacity to look forward with expectancy. The
freedom to change is a vital characteristic. By this means
we treat our present structures carefully and our traditions
lovingly. We respect our forebears from whom we have
received them. We also hold them lightly for they are only

there in order to aid and abet the ongoing process of life and are therefore stamped by provisionality. God's true Church thanks Him for its past traditions. It also knows that not everything will be fulfilled in these present days. It rests secure in the conviction that tomorrow is also God's.

10

God's Discerning Man

Discernment is mature grace. It combines the capacity to pick up unseen spiritual signals with the ability to rightly interpret them. It is a unique quality in which charism and character combine. No spiritual gift has value if it is divorced from love, gentleness and self control. Discernment totally ceases to operate in their absence. Sinful Christians are like estranged sons wandering far from their father's household. They never enjoy incisive perceptions until they have come back to Father again in repentance and renewed faith. The sharpness of our insight and its accuracy therefore becomes a fair barometer for our true spiritual condition.

We should be clear that it is much more than a characteristic reserved for the introspective. A study of the people of God whose lives are described in Scripture makes it clear that it is not confined to those who are of one psychological type. Moses for example, was a gifted spiritual giant, though prone on occasion to bouts of depression and self-doubt. Yet his discernment was accurate and even outstandingly prophetic about unseen future events. Numbers 11.29 is but one instance of this. 'I wish that all the Lord's people were prophets and that the Lord would put His Spirit on them', he says anticipating the events of Pentecost centuries in advance of the day. Although at the end of his life he was sadly deceived by pride, Jehoshaphat is another example. Earlier on his understanding of the ways of God was such that the fortunes of God's people were dramatically changed for the better. From 2 Chronicles 20.20 and onward we are told the story. Enemies can be defeated by the strategy of faith combined with enthusiastic praise. The bluff Peter was never given to despondency, yet it was to him that very significant new understanding is given more than once. So we could go on but it is enough to show that there are many gifts of wisdom available to a wide range of people whatever their circumstances, natures or needs.

In this last chapter we are to consider the cultivation of discernment. Our standard for this is set best of all in the person of God's most perceptive man, Jesus. There are attitudes of heart and spirit which determine our reception of the gift element. There are also habits of mind and action which will affect its growth. Perhaps it was the obvious accuracy of Christ's perception which caused early Christians to reflect on His example in the way they did and in the way in which they urge us to do. Certainly He teaches us more about its development than anyone else.

Receiving Discernment

We need to observe the *wholesomeness of Christ* as the starting point here. It has a more earthly ring about it and to that extent it is more helpful to us struggling mortals, than to speak of His holiness. Yet wholesomeness absorbs holiness. The words *kadosh* in the Old Testament and *hagios* in the New Testament carry the sense of cutting off from the profane and separating to the sacred. They were applied to people, places and things that were regularly used for God. For that reason the holy becomes other than human. It speaks of the presence of God that strikes us with awe and even terror, as Isaiah experienced in the Temple (Isaiah 6.1–9). Important as this otherness of God is, yet in Jesus it is incarnated in the warmth of a vibrant human personality who is manifestly fulfilled in himself and totally aware of the needs of others. The Holy One of God is a whole man and a healthy man.

Jesus comes to us through Scriptures as a whole man

because He refused to compartmentalise life. Clearly He observed the natural processes of growth in trees and plants, and flowers and grass and used them to illustrate His teaching. Building operations, the activities of the military, the tensions of family life, the use and abuse of money and many other aspects of every day life attracted His attention. Children were drawn to Him, as His disciples discovered. They earned His rebuke because of their lack of understanding about His interests in the infants (see Matthew 19.14). He was obviously at ease in the presence of those whom others thought of as sinners. He quite delighted in kicking over the traces set by the narrowed minds of the traditionally religious. There was also a notable freedom about His contact with women, although never once a suggestion of impropriety. They felt safe with Him. For Him the whole of life was lived in an awareness of the presence and power of His Father. The sacred and the secular are combined beneath His perceptive care. With all of this He sought and maintained periods of silence in the midst of much hectic pressure. By this means as He sought and found His Father His spiritual batteries were recharged for the work which lay ahead of Him. On occasions this meant an early rise in order to pray quietly by Himself (Mark 1.35). On others, before taking critical decisions like the choice of the twelve, He spent a whole night praying (Luke 6.12).

We can begin to receive God's wisdom by more Christianity but less religion. Peter Ledger is a friend of mine from Bedford who pastors a fast growing Baptist church. He is a gifted preacher and counsellor. He and I have travelled overseas together in Christian ministry. I am fascinated by the way in which He gets some of his most perceptive sermons. It is not without Bible study but it is not confined to that. One day he was digging his garden and heard the voice which must have been God's telling him to redig a patch already tackled. In spite of threatening rain he did so, though in view of the acres of weedy untackled borders, could scarely see the reason why. 'Dig it again' he was told. So again he tackled it, putting the spade in even deeper this time. Then there it was – the parable for the church that brought everything to the light. A deep twisted mass of ground elder roots just below the surface of the normal dig but full of threat and trouble to any future plans for flowers there. To receive discernment we need to baptise the ordinary elements of life into Christ. The air, the skies, the weather, the earth, bricks and mortar, roads, traffic – our food, crowds on the streets or at the station, our TV and relaxation will all become sensitised by the Spirit. God will say so much to us through all these ways, particularly through the silent things of His own creation.

We notice that Christ also received wisdom by the *givenness of grace*. He confesses this and others observe it. 'Do not believe me unless I do what my Father does. But if I do it, even though you do not believe me, believe the miracles that you may learn and understand that the Father is in me and I in the Father' (John 10.38). He says to explain his actions. Others notice the same things and are stumbled by it all. 'Is this not Jesus, the Son of Joseph, whose father and mother we know?' they complain in John 6.42. 'Where did this man get his wisdom?' they enquire in Matthew 13.53. 'And these miraculous powers?' (Matthew 13.53). For discernment is the fruit of keeping healthy company with God and receiving more of His Spirit. The Holy Spirit is the source of all our spiritual gifts. His comings are not to be taken for granted however. Each fresh experience is clearly defined by a fresh sense of anointing and insight. When Paul encountered Elymas the Jewish Sorcerer in Cyprus he knew immediately he was up against a powerful opponent to the Gospel who would withstand his ministry as much as possible. Paul's discernment came through a fresh infilling of the Spirit and so does ours. For our Heavenly Father goes on giving the Spirit as we go on receiving Him moment by moment (Acts 13. 9).

It is wise to distinguish between wisdom that is God given and psychic perceptions. The former come to us through strong relationships born and cherished by the Holy Spirit.

The latter is only striking because of the odd phenomena with which it is accociated. Some years ago I came across a young woman whose skills owed more to the psychic than the spiritual. She described what she saw and heard in order to minister helpfully to others, and it was all disturbingly accurate. Words written over their faces, verses suddenly emerging from Scripture, demonic powers visible on the shoulders of the demonised were only a part of her experience. We met in a church in Ilfracombe where our family was on holiday with Tony McQueen and his family. Tony and I had left our wives and children behind to go for a quiet Sunday evening service together. The young woman was waiting for us. Armed to the teeth with perceptive prophecies she frightened us both to death. But never once in the New Testament is this sort of experience commended. For she did not manifest any compassion or grace as she shared her revelations. In the end we took little notice of them but did our best to encourage her to grow her gifts in other ways. God's people get their wisdom as Christ did. An intimate Father gives special insight to faithful children who come to Him for it.

Growing in Discernment

Whilst pure wisdom comes to us from above it is also ours as we mature spiritually. We are given an insight into Christ's experience of this process in the fascinating account of His childhood in Luke 2.41–52. We have already looked at this incident but it bears some further thought. He was twelve years of age at the time and visiting Jerusalem at Passover. He was approaching His Bar Mitzvah, the time when a boy could join the religious life of Israel as a son of the commandments. Having missed Him on the return journey north after the festival, His distraught parents returned to the city, finding Him in the temple courts totally absorbed in discussion with the teachers. His reply to their understandable rebuke is not an example of adolescent cheek. It shows the developing independence of the discerning mind.

'Why were you searching for me?' He asked. 'Didn't you know that I had to be in my Father's house?' For discerning people weigh things for themselves in the light of their relationship with God. Nevertheless there is the other side. For the account goes on to describe the return to mundane Nazareth. It was a hard town then, and as events have shown, a hard place subsequently. But Jesus was obedient to His parents there and 'grew in wisdom and stature and favour with God and men.' We grow as we find ourselves in relation to our Father and are fully reconciled to our circumstances too.

Restlessness is a real enemy to the process. It means that we are not content with the learning programme that Father has set us because we always know better. It may be a sign of foolish ambition. 'Cromwell, I charge thee, fling away ambition, by that sin fell the angels,' Cardinal Wolsey is made to say by Shakespeare. That is the desire to get for ourselves what God has given to another and would never entrust us with. It can be the squirming of a sin laden conscience that stubbornly chooses the harshness of guilt to the joy of forgiveness. If we want to grow up it is wise to learn to lie down and rest in the goodness of a God who cares.

In Luke's account we move swiftly from Christ's boyhood and His baptism to another major stage in the growth process. It is that of the struggle through spiritual testing which Christ experienced with the devil and in the deserts (Luke 4.1–13). The various specific attacks Jesus repulsed are important to understand. Stones to bread (Luke 4.3) is the temptation to use spiritual power for selfish ends. It may go further than that as John Howard Yoder suggests, to include the economic option. Provide a massive banquet and you will be king. The kingdoms and the world and their glory at the worship of Satan speaks of the short cut to final victory without the humiliation of the cross. Then the pinnacle of the temple experience, of miraculous powers for spectacular ends, and Jesus resisted these notions with Scriptural insight. For the whole experience ends signific-

antly. 'When the devil had finished all this tempting, he left
him until an opportune time' (Luke 4.13).

We grow in discernment as we understand the strategies
of Satan, a wily foe. Christ's dealings with him were unique
to Him, but also significant for us. How often we find
ourselves involved in the same struggles to the same ends.
The issues at stake are always to do with salvation, sonship
and service. It is only inasmuch as we perceive what Satan
is about, and how his enticements are directed towards our
departure from Christ that we overcome them. We must add
that our own intrinsic sinful perversity gives Satan abundant
spiritual leverage. Yet in a remarkable way, the experience
of his attacks should indicate to us our greatest personal
vulnerability and thus the places where Christ's protection
is most required. If we are constantly being tempted into
greater insecurity or avarice or lust then this says enough
to us to indicate the way we should respond to it all. We
are not to succumb to defeatism by repeated experiences of
this sort. But confession, repentance and disciplined living
and much prayer are called for. Cultivating the devotional
life is the answer to spiritual onslaughts. For temptation is
not to be seen as a negative experience but one that is filled
with promise. Having negotiated the trial safely Luke tells
us 'Jesus returned to Galilee in the power of the Holy
Spirit and news about Him spread throughout the whole
countryside' (Luke 4.14). If we have perceived how the foe
moves, and where and why he attackes as he does we will
fly for refuge to our shepherd and guardian who is coven-
anted to keep us from falling.

Reflecting Discernment

Jesus manifested His understanding of God and His ways
by a matchless sense of timing. We know all about the futile
blusterings of His disciples including those of the inner core
of Peter, James and John. How often have we all identified
with them as we have reflected on some of our wayward
reactions to people or circumstances. But Jesus never put a

foot wrong. Clearly, His whole life was governed by a powerful sense of destiny. It also affected His daily activities. 'My hour has not yet come' He declares in Cana prior to the first miracle there (John 2.4). He refuses to agree to the suggestions of His brothers about a journey to Jerusalem at the Feast of Tabernacles for the same reason (John 7.10). Subsequently however, He knows that the hour is right, even for the drama of redemption through His cross. 'What shall I say? Father save me from this hour? No, for this very reason I came to this hour' (John 12.27). For wisdom decrees not only the appropriate word for every situation but also a correct measure of the capacity of others to receive it. Did His sense of timing cause Jesus to bite His tongue from time to time? We don't know the answer to that question, but if we are growing in perception we will know it well for ourselves. Or the Holy Spirit will check us in another way. We will be more careful with our words and more controlled in our judgements. Instead of going in like the poverbial bull in the china shop, we will have seen how 'a soft answer turns away wrath'! Or the answer may be non-verbally communicated. That calm and measured gaze of Jesus when He was held at the High Priest's home but catches Peter's eye in the courtyard outside when he is in the full flow of his denials is just right. 'And the Lord turned and looked on Peter . . . and Peter remembered the word . . .' (Luke 23.61). A kind friend once cautioned me over one of my more impetuous declarations. 'There is more than one way to skin a rabbit, Douglas.' Yes, he was right, and the way I was proposing was not the best. I regret my intemperate outbursts and realise the need to learn how best to express convictions with integrity combined with care. 'A word aptly spoken is like apples of gold in settings of silver' says Proverbs 25.11. 'Let your conversation be always full of grace, seasoned with salt, so that you may know how to answer everyone' says Paul (Colossians 4.6). Our speech reveals our true understanding of these things not by magnifying the dulling qualities of guardedness and reserve but by exhibiting those of grace and scintillating faith in God.

Christ's skill is demonstrated in so many other areas. Clearly He reads people, especially those close to Him. To draw close to Christ is to invite His scrutiny, as the disciples discover. He has the same insight with others also, Herodians, Zealots, Pharisees, Sadducees, and even Romans. This is seen most clearly in the fascinating interview between Jesus and Pilate recorded in the Gospels (John 18.33 – 19.16). As is always the case with Him, Jesus is in charge of the conversation. Technically, He is on trial but it is soon evident that it is Pilate's conscience that is in the dock before a wonderfully perceptive and generous Judge. As if to help Pilate off the hook on which he would soon hang himself by passing the crucial judgement Jesus said to him 'You would have no power over me if it had not been given you from above. Therefore the one who handed me over to you is guilty of a greater sin' (John 19.11).

Yet, to return again to Christ's positive use of natural elements, He also perceives the word God brings to Him, speaking through the swaying of the grass in the fields and the birds in the air. We grow in discernment as we develop sensitivity to the tones of God in creation and the space of God in the open skies. All of our ministry so far has been in an urban setting. The rural beauty of Britain has attracted us all the more so, because we do not see it every day. When we moved house recently we asked God to give us a place of quietness and also a home with an open aspect. For months we pursued one false lead followed by another. Always they were to homes just beyond our budget and we only examined them because we had allowed our faith to assume a somewhat desperate quality. This is always the price you pay for following hectic faith teaching. Then at the last moment God stepped in to help us. At the time we had moved out of one house and were staying in quite unsuitable accommodation – a manse half modernised by a minister with neither the time nor the skills nor the cash for the proper job. We now find ourselves still living in the inner suburbs, but at the top of a hill and the views God has given us! We can see the North Downs in one direction and the centre of London in another. We overlook a vast area of the city that sparkles like a brilliant Christmas tree in the dusk at night. And those open skies! To learn to look up to the heavens and beyond them, to the Lord who is above all is a key to spiritual growth. To talk to Him in praise and adoration leads us to share our conflicts and our fears and our hopes with Him. I enjoy prayer in the open air and He loves to speak to me then when I am out walking. The word is usually heard inwardly, but is often accompanied by a gentle breath of wind caressing the face like a touch from heaven. We need to get alone with God in order to hear Him. We must learn to spend time with Him and give Him room if we are to know and feel His presence. When we do so we will see secrets long since hidden from the eyes of others. Even the angels will be enquiring about God's personal conversations with us.

There is also His skill in reading current events accurately. His word about the Temple is one example. 'Not one stone left upon another' must have seemed an outrageous prophecy at the time. Similarly, when He spoke about the city of Jerusalem surrounded by armies and trampled down 'until the time of the Gentiles are fulfilled' (Luke 24.24). At the very least these words show that Jesus took an active interest in everyday affairs. He wanted to be accurately informed. Then in addition He also anticipated the future with extraordinary accuracy. Events become concertina-ed by His word. The trials which broke forth in the time of the Jewish revolt in AD70, stand hard against those that still await fulfilment at the end of the age. To hear Him speak at all will be to hear Him speak about what is and what will be. Our corporate failure to discern in the Church today has bound and fettered the Church to its present day society. We are gagged when it comes to speaking about the directions to follow in the future because we have emphasised history and so ignored the ministry of prophecy that we have handed it over to the unstable as their own hunting ground. In Bombay, India there is a mighty monument called the Gateway to India that was built in honour of King George V and Queen Mary on the occasion of their visit in 1911 as Emperor and Empress of India. Having seen this imposing edifice one wonders why it is that the Church could not read the signs of the times regarding India as accurately as Mahatma Gandhi did a few years later. We can now see that the age of the British Empire is well and truly past and gone for ever. A discerning church in our age will know how to apply God's enduring principles of morality, generosity, integrity and faith to immediate political problems and thus will speak relevantly to the age. It is discernment which preserves the Church from becoming spiritually moribund in an age that needs to hear God speak.

The Fruits of Discernment

Like Jesus, God's discerning people are truly free in their own spirits. 'A Christian is a perfectly free lord of all, subject to none. A Christian is a perfectly dutiful servant of all, subject to all', says Martin Luther. Since they are able to read life in its complexities, and people in their strange reactions, and God in His faithfulness, they are no man's slave. The mark of discernment is carefreeness. The discerning know that none can harm them since they belong to Christ. They are released from tension and despair, also from the twin imposters of triumph and disaster. They hate nothing but sin and fear no one but God.

God's good purposes no longer surprise them. For they are released from an eschatology of despair at the end. To be sure God is never in a rush. As to how exactly He will fulfil those apparently contradictory purposes of His to unite His Church and yet to make His Church pure remains a mystery. But it is enough to know that He can and will achieve this somehow. Mystery is part of deity and must remain part of our religion. It is because Christians lack discernment that they become impatient for the purposes of God and wish to hasten on the process. Inevitably they either pursue the purity of the Church at the expense of the unity of the Church or vice versa and cannot seem to combine both desirable ends. Perhaps they feel that God could still be defeated in the end by the devil, a lie, or an apostate church. But this will never be. The book of Revelation concludes with the vision of God's New Jerusalem descending out of heaven from God as a bride ready for her husband. The mark of true discernment is always that of strong confidence in God's sovereignty.

Earlier on we distinguished between discernment and suspicion. This much needed Christian gift and much neglected Christian ministry produces a much needed blessing among Christians. For to know all is also to understand all. It is the first step towards forgiving all. Far from producing a company of carping Christians eager to expose each other's faults it develops the grace of merciful love among the people of God. For we have seen enough of ourselves to know the need for it. We have seen sufficient of others to know their willingness to grant it. Even when discernment brings us to a crisis requiring firm action, in truth we remember mercy.

Suggestions for Further Reading

Chapter 1.	*Dynamics of the Spiritual Life*	Richard Lovelace (Paternoster Press)
	Bursting the Wineskins	Michael Cassidy (Hodder)
Chapter 2.	*Article on* Diakrisis	Theological Word Book of the N.T. Vol III. G. Kittel
	Gifts & Graces	Arnold Bittlinger (Hodder)
	Gifts & Ministries	Arnold Bittlinger (Hodder)
	I Believe in the Holy Spirit	Michael Green (Hodder)
Chapter 3.	*Jesus and the Kingdom*	G.E. Ladd (SPCK)
	Signs & Wonders Today	Donald Bridge (IVP)
	Rediscovering the Spirit	Rob Warner (Hodder)
	Resting in the Spirit	John Richards (pamphlet)
Chapter 4.	*Healing*	Francis McNutt (Ave Maria Press)
	Rediscovering Healing	Francis McNutt (Ave Maria Press)
	Prayers for Inner Healing	Robert Faricy (SCM)
	Power Evangelism	John Wimber (Hodder)
Chapter 5.	*But deliver us from Evil*	John Richards (DLT)
	I Believe in Satan's Downfall	M. Green (Hodder)
	Biblical Demonology	M. Unger (Scripture Press)
	Christ and the Powers	H. Berkhof (Herald Press)
Chapter 6.	*Let the Bible Speak*	J. Balchin (IVP)
	A Users' Guide to the Bible	C. Wright (Lion)

	Restoring the Kingdom	A. Walker (Hodder)
Chapter 7.	*New Testament Prophecy*	D. Hill (Marshalls)
	Prophecy	B. Yocum (Servant Books)
	A Narration of Surprising Conversions	J. Edwards (Banner of Truth)
Chapter 8.	*Reflected Glory*	T.A. Smail (Hodder)
	The Forgotten Father	T.A. Smail (Hodder)
Chapter 9.	*The Church*	Hans Kung (Search)
	Paul's Idea of Community	R. Banks (Paternoster)
	I Believe in the Church	D. Watson (Hodder)
	The Politics of Jesus	J.H. Yoder (Eardman)
	The Mustard Seed Conspiracy	Tom Sine (Marc Europe)
Chapter 10.	*Celebration of Discipline*	R. Foster (Hodder)
	Money, Sex & Power	R. Foster (Hodder)
	Jesus & the Spirit	J.D.G. Dunn (SCM)
	Reflected Glory	T.A. Smail (Hodder)